Susse...
Best Pub Walks
Arundel to Robertsbridge

Jonny Young

S.B. Publications

First published in 2010 by S. B. Publications
Tel: 01323 893498
Email: sbpublications@tiscali.co.uk
www.sbpublications.co.uk

ISBN 978-1-85770-358-0

Designed and Typeset by EH Graphics (01273) 515527

CONTENTS

SUSSEX

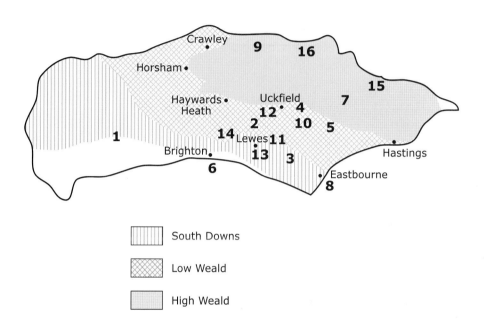

Crawley

Horsham

Haywards Heath

Uckfield

Lewes

Brighton

Hastings

Eastbourne

9 16

15

7

12 4

2 10 5

14 11

1

13 3

6

8

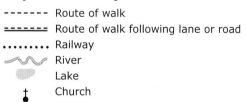

South Downs

Low Weald

High Weald

Key to walk maps

------- Route of walk
======= Route of walk following lane or road
••••••••• Railway
⌇⌇⌇ River
Lake
✝ Church

INTRODUCTION

There is something rather pleasing about circular walks; perhaps it is the sense of completeness, or the simple fact of not needing to retrace one's steps for any great distance. This collection contains 16 such walks, exploring Sussex landscapes from riverside and reservoir to woodland and rolling field, with the opportunity to discover unique vistas, historic houses, old railway lines and tucked-away villages.

The walks range between 2-5 miles in length and all can be easily tackled as part of a leisurely afternoon stroll either before or after a visit to a Sussex pub. Most require very little in the way of steep ascents and those that do (particularly at Glynde, Berwick and the longer route at Eastbourne) are carefully chosen so that there are excellent views to make regular pausing a highlight rather than a hindrance.

Along the way, brief insights into the area have been provided in order to enhance the appreciation of the walk; equally it is hoped they will provide some interest and enjoyment to the armchair reader. Cumulatively, the walks pass no fewer than twenty Grade I listed buildings, from churches to castles, but also including residences such as Swanborough Manor near Lewes and Kipling's residence at Bateman's in Burwash. Often, part of the route joins one of the many long distance footpaths passing through the county, such as the South Downs Way (Eastbourne and Berwick), Wealdway (Withyham, East Hoathly and Eastbourne), Vanguard Way (Berwick and Blackboys), 1066 Country Walk (Boreham Street) and Sussex Border Path (East Grinstead).

Sussex has many 'icons', perhaps the most well-known and most photographed being the Seven Sisters and Beachy Head cliffs. To many locals, however, it is a pint of the local beer, Harveys Sussex Best, that is as synonymous with the notion of 'Sussex' as Brighton Rock, chalk coastlines and the rolling hills of the South Downs, and in this particular collection all the walks have been designed around a visit to a Harveys pub to allow the reader and walker to enjoy not only the local countryside, but also the local tipple. Should readers choose to enjoy the walk by itself, perhaps with a picnic lunch, details of alternative parking are provided. Pub opening times have been omitted purely as an accurate rendering of each of the variations not only between weekdays and weekends, but also seasonally, would in some cases fill an entire page on their own. Weekend walkers should have no cause for concern, but those wanting to try a Tuesday afternoon ramble in winter may be advised to phone ahead using the contact details provided!

Sketch maps, with the exception of Brighton, have been reproduced with an approximate scale of 1: 25 000 to allow readers to correlate them with the relevant Ordnance Survey map and area. Regular six figure OS waypoints are also included to enable readers using OS maps or GPS devices to follow the route easily. To the best of my knowledge all information contained herein is correct, but if the reader spots any changes since these walks were written, or has any further insights, I would be delighted to hear from them via twitter.com/sussexbestwalks, where there are also additional photographs and resources.

For this collection I am indebted firstly to Harveys, particularly Zoe Prescott, Bill Inman and Hamish Elder, for their advice, fact-checking and supplying of the images found on pages 1, 9-12 and 109. I am also indebted to my family for instilling me with a love of walking and without whom this book would have been impossible.

By no means is this intended as a definitive collection of Sussex walks; rather, it is hoped they will give a brief, but enjoyable, insight into the varied nature of the Sussex countryside and provoke the reader's own exploration around the county which, despite being one of the most populated parts of the UK, remains so pleasantly unspoilt. Long may it remain so!

I hope you enjoy these walks as much as I have compiling them.

Jonny Young, May 2010

WHAT IS HARVEYS?

To many, Harveys Brewery is as synonymous with the notion of 'Sussex' as Brighton Rock, chalk coastlines and the rolling hills of the South Downs. Established in 1790 and today producing some 45 000 barrels (equivalent to nearly 13 million pints) each year, Harveys is both the oldest and largest independent brewery in the county. It's also one of the most popular: in 2007 Harveys' signature beer, Sussex Best, was voted the 'Favourite beer in South & South East England' in a public ballot of the nation's pubs conducted by Cask Marque and the Daily Telegraph, coming runner-up only to London Pride in the London area as well.

Perhaps most striking, however, is Harveys' unusually close affinity with the county in which it is brewed. Unlike many beers, which can often be found across the country, Harveys operates predominantly within a sixty-mile distribution radius of its brewery in Lewes: tourists wishing to try Harveys Sussex Best, which makes up almost 90% of the brewery's production, will probably need to visit Sussex to do so.

By choosing to distribute primarily within Sussex, the brewery can remain both economical and environmentally friendly as the majority of casks and bottles can be returned and reused. Alongside this, all by-products such as spent grains and hops are returned to local agriculture, both saving money on disposal and lessening landfill.
In recognition of this attitude, in 2005 Harveys won the South East England Development Agency (SEEDA) medium-sized Sustainable Business Award, making it one of the greenest businesses between Oxford and Dover.

Remaining a family-run business, Harveys is still produced in The Bridge Wharf Brewery, Lewes over 200 years since Georgian wine merchant John Harvey first started brewing as a sideline to his wine and brandy shipping business. To this day, no-one knows for certain if he bears any relation to the John Harvey who established a famous brand of sherry in 1838 - apparently very unlikely.

As well as supplying around 400 freehouses in Sussex, Harveys operates 47 pubs - from bustling town locals to country retreats. These offer the perfect opportunity to experience the real 'flavour of Sussex' by enjoying a drink of locally-brewed beer accompanied by a hearty meal made from fresh local produce. And what better way to whet the appetite than with a walk exploring the gloriously varied Sussex countryside, be it riverside, coast, downland or woodland?

THROUGH THE SEASONS

The countryside holds interest whatever the season: in spring many of the woodlands are full of bluebells and wood anemones, in summer the trees are in full leaf, in early autumn the fields are full of crops and in winter the bare trees often provide the best views. Aside from the permanent fixture of the multi-award-winning Sussex Best, there are many Harveys beers which are only available on draught in certain calendar months, providing the perfect opportunity to visit the pubs and explore the walks all year round. Here is a selection:

SPRING

Porter 4.8% - MARCH

Porters developed in London in the 18th century and were so called due to their popularity among the street and river porters working in Billingsgate and Smithfield markets. Harveys Porter is brewed from an original porter recipe of 1859 from Henry Harvey's brewing journal, and in 1999 it was chosen as the 'Ultimate Pizza Beer' in the Beauty of Hops awards.
A dark coloured beer with bitter burnt flavours.

Knots of May Light Mild 3% - MAY

First brewed to celebrate the 21st birthday of the eponymous team of women's Morris Dancers, whose name refers to the ancient custom of gathering knots of flowers on May Day. The draught itself is brewed to coincide with the start of the Morris Dancing season and many dances can be seen across the county at this time of year. For more information about the Knots of May team and programme see www.knotsofmay.org.uk
Gentle mild with a deep ruby colour and a delicate hop fragrance.
Also available: Olympia (April)

SUMMER

Copperwheat Beer 4.8% - JUNE
Light in colour with hints of spice in the relatively fruity flavour. Served chilled; perfect for the summer weather!

Tom Paine Ale 5.5% - JULY
Brewed to coincide with the celebration of Independence Day in America, Tom Paine Ale is named after the radical who lived in Lewes in the eighteenth century. Initially an excise officer, he emigrated to Philadelphia in 1774 and published Common Sense, a pro-

independence pamphlet which established him as a revolutionary propagandist. Soon after American independence had been won, Paine returned to Europe and greatly influenced the French Revolution with his Rights of Man in 1791, a guide to Enlightenment ideas. In 1802, at President Jefferson's invitation, he returned to America where he died in 1809. Paine's residence at Bull House, 92 High Street (150 yards from Lewes Castle) is open to the public for guided tours at weekends. For more information see www.lewesguidedwalks.vpweb.co.uk
A premium dry hopped bitter

Armada Ale 4.5% - AUGUST
Despite being available all year round, this golden bitter with a dry, bitter palate and a splendid aroma of hops is particularly appropriate for mid-summer.

AUTUMN

Southdown Harvest 5% - SEPTEMBER
This beer celebrates the time of year that historically has been associated with the gathering in of the harvest. Uses freshly-harvested Sussex Fuggles (a variety of hop) together with spring water to produce a beer that gives a true "taste of the South Downs".

Old Ale 4.3% - OCTOBER

Available from October to May, Old Ale is a soft, full beer with a nutty palate reminiscent of the mild ales produced during the early part of the 20th century. Locals may be heard to ask for a 'Mother-in-Law': half a pint of Old and half a pint of Bitter (Best).

Bonfire Boy 5.8% - NOVEMBER

Harveys first brewed and bottled Bonfire Boy as a tribute to the emergency services, following the fire in July 1996 which destroyed

the brewery shop and offices. As well as providing a continuing tribute to the emergency services, the beer also celebrates the extensive celebrations which take place in Lewes on November 5 and which attract spectators from miles around.

A strong ale with a subtle smoky character
Also available: Star of Eastbourne (October)

WINTER

Christmas Ale 8.1% - DECEMBER

A strong "Barley Wine" brewed to a strength similar to the beers produced by the Tudor brewers in the time of Queen Elizabeth 1, this dark, heavily-hopped beer is an ideal accompaniment to the festive season.

Kiss (4.8%) - FEBRUARY

Despite ostensibly marking St Valentine's Day, Harveys Kiss was in fact first brewed to celebrate the brief return of Rodin's famous marble sculpture *The Kiss* to Lewes in 1999 from where it was

originally commissioned in 1900 (arriving in 1904). One of three full-scale versions of the sculpture made in Rodin's lifetime, *The Kiss* depicts the first embrace of Paolo and Francesca, the adulterous lovers of Dante's Inferno. Second only in popularity to his famous *The Thinker,* Rodin's sculpture is currently housed in the Tate Modern.

An amber-coloured beer, relatively thin and fruity.

There are also many bottled varieties available from behind the bar and from the Harveys shop in Lewes. Harveys has also recently installed a micro brewery which enables the production of small quantities of beers to suit individual requirements.

For more information see www.harveys.org.uk or visit the Harveys shop in Cliffe High Street, Lewes.

Sussex Best 4% -

Winner of the First Prize Gold Medal at the International Brewers' Exhibition in 1980, this beer is brewed to an original gravity of 1036° -1040° from a recipe which has evolved over many years. It is a full, well-hopped bitter with a reputation that exceeds the borders of its native and adjoining counties.
A dark copper-colour bitter with small white head and a complex malty flavour. Available all year.

HARVEYS

WHITE HART

Set in the heart of the attractive historic market town of Arundel, The White Hart is the only pub to be found on the east bank of the River Arun. A friendly welcome is to be found from the relatively new tenants who are in the process of adding a new lounge area at the time of going to press. At present, quirky features include an Underwood portable typewriter, antique sets of scales and bed warmers which adorn the walls alongside pewter tankards and the more ubiquitously-seen dartboard.

The menu includes traditional pub fare with an enjoyable steak, kidney and mushroom pie featuring Harveys ale. Lighter options include a range of sandwiches and baguettes and a hearty all-day breakfast. The White Hart also aims to stock all Harveys seasonal draught ales. For more information call 01903 884 422.

THE WALK

LENGTH: 4 MILES

Predominantly a riverside stroll, the walk winds northwards along the bank of the River Arun, which was once navigable all the way from Littlehampton to London via the River Wey. There are spectacular views of Arundel's Castle and Cathedral before the route passes Swanbourne Lake and climbs briefly through Arundel Park to re-emerge at the top end of the town.

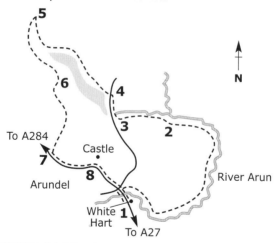

- **OS MAP:**
- Explorer 121: Arundel & Pulborough
- **START POINT:**
- The White Hart (BN18 9JG; grid ref TQ020069)
- **GETTING THERE:**
- Via A27 ten miles west of Worthing. There is limited street parking and a pay-and-display car park in Mill Road (grid ref. TQ021071). The White Hart does not have a car park.
- **PUBLIC TRANSPORT:**
- Stagecoach bus service 700 stops opposite The White Hart and runs half-hourly Mon-Sat towards Worthing and Brighton. Arundel railway station (BN18 9PH) is served by trains between Bognor Regis and London Victoria.

1. Cross the bridge over the River Arun and turn right along Mill Road, turning right again almost immediately into **Jubilee Gardens.** Just to the left of a sign for Arundel Boatyard, follow a narrow path by the side of Riverside Tea Gardens, passing the boatyard itself to emerge along the top of the riverbank. From here, the route traces the meanders of the Arun, heading first eastwards before bending northwards. Ignore a footpath turning on the left (TQ028071).

In Jubilee Gardens are the remains of a Dominican Priory, founded in the 13th century, which suffered from the Dissolution of the Monasteries in 1538.

2. When the river heads northwards for the second time, pass through a kissing gate and over a small channel on the left (TQ024077). Turn left almost immediately afterwards to follow the right-hand side of this channel on a narrow, partially-surfaced path leading back to Mill Road. On the right is the perimeter fence of the **Wildfowl and Wetlands Trust Reserve.**

The Wildfowl & Wetlands Trust (WWT) is a leading UK conservation organisation founded in 1946 by the naturalist and artist, the late Sir Peter Scott, and has a national network of nine specialist wetland visitor centres. Arundel Wetland Centre contains 64 acres of wetland habitats housing wildfowl from around the globe.

3. The path emerges by two bridges; ignoring the first of these, follow steps up to the small road bridge. Turn right along Mill Road for a few yards to reach Swanbourne Lodge tearooms by the edge of **Swanbourne Lake.**

Swanbourne Lake is a former mill pond, now a popular recreation site with rowing facilities and plenty of seats to watch the many species of wildfowl that visit here. The mill, demolished in the 1840s, featured in John Constable's last painting in 1837.

4. The path continues along the right-hand side of the lake and winds briefly uphill. **Hiorne Tower,** which will be passed later, can soon be seen high on the ridge to the left. At the head of the lake, ignore a footpath leading off to the left and continue ahead over a stile by a gate towards the centre of the valley bottom.

5. On meeting a junction of paths from two other dry valleys (TQ011086), turn left and double back uphill, briefly above the path just traversed.

The path below Hiorne Tower is part of the Monarch's Way, a 615-mile long-distance footpath based on the approximate route of Charles II's escape in 1651 after having lost to Cromwell at the Battle of Worcester. Our walk now follows this route back to the White Hart, but the Monarch's Way itself continues on to Shoreham, from where Charles made his escape.

6. After passing through a gate at the top of the hill above Mill Hanger (the word 'Hanger' denoting a woodland 'hanging' on the hillside and its prefix recalling the mill which was once situated here), turn immediately right up an embankment to reach training gallops.

Racehorse gallops above Mill Hanger.

7. Cross the gallops and directly over the parkland in front of Hiorne tower, in fact a triangular folly, towards a surfaced drive through **Arundel Park.** On reaching the drive (TQ013080), turn left and follow it through the park entrance to a main road running along the top of the town. Keep the wall of Arundel Park on the left and walk past **Arundel Cathedral** and **St Nicholas' Church.**

The Anglican Church of St Nicholas is housed in the same building as the Roman Catholic Fitzalan Chapel on the border of the castle grounds, making it the only church of its kind in England.

8. Continue past the castle as the road bears round to the right (TQ018072), with a view down into the centre of Arundel itself, today mostly nestled at the foot of the hill. On the right, the Town Hall can be glimpsed down Maltravers Street, revealing this to be the original centre of the town; indeed this was the original road to Chichester. The following street on the right, Tarrant Street, owes its name to the original Celtic name for the river. Ahead, keep to the left side of the war memorial to emerge by the post office by the mini-roundabout at the junction with Mill Road. Cross straight ahead over the bridge to return to The White Hart.

ARUNDEL AT A GLANCE

Arundel Castle, set in 40 acres of sweeping grounds and gardens, was first built in 1068 as a motte and bailey structure by Roger de Montgomery, Earl of Arundel. The gatehouse followed in 1070. The castle houses a fascinating collection of fine furniture dating from the 16th century and portraits by Van Dyck, Gainsborough, Reynolds and Canaletto. Queen Victoria visited in 1846.

From the late 1700s until the late 1800s, there was considerable commercial traffic on the River Arun and through the Wey and Arun canal to Guildford and the Thames (closed in 1871 but currently being partially renovated).

By 1791 ships of 200 tons could reach Arundel, where goods were transferred to sailing barges to travel upriver. Like many waterways, the barges lost out to the railway.

Six miles north of Arundel nestling in the foothills of the South Downs lies Bignor Roman Villa, first excavated in 1811 and featuring Roman mosaics and the remains of a hypocaust, a Roman underfloor heating system.

• • • • • • • • • •

From the riverbank there are good views of Arundel Cathedral, St Nicholas' Church and Arundel Castle, all situated at the top of the town on a dip slope of the South Downs.

WALK 2   BARCOMBE

ROYAL OAK

Situated in a quiet village near the once-canalized River Ouse, this 16th century pub has been owned by Mike and Caroline Austen for over 25 years. There are tables and attractive hanging baskets at the front which make for pleasant summer visiting, but the snug interior is also enjoyable in the colder months and remains a centre of the community. Inside there is also a function room and, more intriguingly, a skittle alley available for hire for groups.

Adorning the walls are an informative wine display cabinet and paintings of Sussex landscapes; on the author's last visit an attractive calendar entitled 'The Sussex Year' was also available for purchase.

Food includes rump of Sussex lamb and an enjoyable, and popular, Sunday roast. A charity quiz is held on the last Tuesday of the month.

For more information see www.royal-oakbarcombe.co.uk or call 01273 400 418.

THE WALK

LENGTH: 4 MILES

Criss-crossing through fields and along country lanes, this walk investigates the original location of Barcombe village, passes close to the river Ouse and meets the route of the now dismantled railway line from Lewes-East Grinstead.

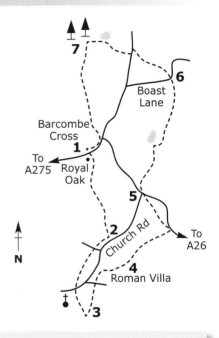

- **OS MAP:**
  Explorer 122: Brighton & Hove
- **START POINT:**
  The Royal Oak (BN8 5BA; grid ref TQ420157)
- **GETTING THERE:**
  Barcombe is situated about five miles north of Lewes and can be reached via A275, or via A26 from Uckfield. There is limited street parking and a small public car park beside the post office (grid ref TQ 420158). The Royal Oak does not have a car park.
- **PUBLIC TRANSPORT:**
  An infrequent bus service is operated by Countryliner 125 between Barcombe and Alfriston via Lewes. The nearest railway station is at Cooksbridge (BN7 3QG).

1. Emerging from the pub, take the narrow lane down its right-hand side and continue ahead over a crossroad onto **Mongers Lane.** The route shortly bears right onto a narrow enclosed tarmac footpath to emerge in the corner of a field. Follow the right-hand boundary downhill with a broad expanse of Sussex downland visible to the left. At the bottom of the hill, cross a stile and turn sharply left by the edge of a hedgerow to walk along a grassy embankment which once carried the Lewes-East Grinstead railway line between 1882 and 1958. Follow the path as it bears right down a slope and under a power line towards a kissing gate on the edge of woodland, passing through this to emerge in a small field. Turn left along the field boundary. A few paces beyond the far corner, cross a stile (TQ422151) and head towards an oak tree in the right-hand boundary of the adjacent field. Beyond this, a stile leads into a further field, through which the path bears diagonally left to reach **Church Road.**

2. Turn right along the lane and, when it forks by a white weather-boarded house opposite a post box, turn right and then almost immediately left into a field behind the house itself. Follow the left-hand boundary of two fields to emerge onto a lane by Barcombe Church. Cross the lane onto a drive leading to the church itself, veering left through a wide wooden gate just before its entrance. Pass through two small pastures, in the second of which the path heads diagonally left.

3. Over a small footbridge in the bottom corner (TQ420142), turn left and almost double back along a wide track to the left of an arable field. On reaching a lane leading to **Culver Farm,** maintain direction onto a narrow drive to the left of an isolated house. When this curves right towards the

Footpath sign by Barcombe Church.

house itself, continue ahead on a narrow hedge-enclosed footpath which bears right over a small pasture into a field. Cross diagonally left towards a ditch halfway along the left-hand boundary, skirting to the left of excavations for a Roman villa.

Embankment marking the line of the Lewes-East Grinstead railway. From this vantage point it is also possible to see the route of the old Lewes-Uckfield line with Barcombe Mills station visible to the north.

4. By a clear signpost, pass into the adjacent field and walk ahead towards and over a grassy embankment (TQ424148). Over this, cross a bridge and follow a series of small fields reaching a road just after passing a **WWII pillbox** (TQ428150). Do not cross the stile leading to the road itself, but turn left up a short rise, at the top of which the path bears diagonally right, aiming to the left of a black-roofed barn. Pass through a gap in the fence on the right-hand side, marked by black-coated posts, and maintain direction, heading diagonally to the top corner of the field beyond. Cross a stile and turn right to rejoin the road at a T-junction (TQ425154).

5. Bear left and then turn almost immediately right onto a concrete drive leading to the black-roofed barn seen earlier. Skirt round the right-hand edge of this and follow a track to the left of the farmhouse with the Ouse visible away to the right. Just after the track bears round to the right, take a signed path (TQ427156) heading downhill towards a small reservoir. At the bottom, turn right over a stile and shortly cross a bridge over a river channel, after which the path follows the edge of fields, keeping the meander of the river on the left. In the third of these, ignore a path leading diagonally right (TQ429163) and head uphill towards the red brick building of Banks Farm. On meeting the driveway, turn left to meet a bend in Boast Lane at **Clay Corner.**

6. Maintain direction over a stile into a small field and pass to the right of an attractive barn at **Scobell's Farm.** Beyond this, a gate leads into a sloping meadow. Descend this diagonally right, passing through a gap in the hedge and over a small stream to ascend the right-hand edge of the field beyond. In the top corner the route leads along a narrow enclosed path between houses to emerge onto a country lane (TQ425168). Turn left and then after 50 yards right onto a concrete drive signposted Knowlands Farm and Granary. Walk downhill, passing a large pond and attractive farm buildings to reach a field gate on the edge of **Knowlands Wood.**

7. Immediately before the gate, turn left (TQ419169) and walk along the edge of a field with a hedgerow on the right and Barcombe Cross visible ahead. Maintain direction as the path passes along the left-hand side of the field beyond, over a concrete bridge crossing the **Bevern Stream** and uphill along the edge of two further fields to emerge onto a lane. Follow the lane as it bears round to the left in front of a recreation ground to arrive at a small roundabout in the centre of Barcombe Cross. Turn right and the Royal Oak is a few yards away on the left.

Barn at Scobell's Farm

BARCOMBE AT A GLANCE

Barcombe church

- 'Barcombe' itself is situated slightly to the south of the village in which the walk begins, which is strictly named Barcombe Cross. The villagers of the 'original' Barcombe evacuated during the Medieval plague. Most people know the new village by the name of Barcombe, however, and only on maps is its full name given.

- The fertile Ouse valley has provided ideal barley-growing conditions for centuries and the village name originally began as 'Bere camp' from the Anglo Saxon 'bere', meaning barley; thus 'barley camp'.

- A plaque on Pikes bridge just beyond Barcombe Mills shows that this was the first road tollgate in the county, built in 1066.

- Barcombe lies near a junction of Ermine Street, the old Roman road from Newhaven to London, and Greensand Way, a link road under the South Downs connecting settlements from Barcombe Mills to Stane Street at Hardham. Remains have been found of a Roman villa and an earlier Iron Age roundhouse.

- For more information about Lewes-Uckfield railway line see Walk 12: Isfield.

•••••••••

BERWICK

CRICKETERS ARMS

Nestling at the foot of the South Downs, this traditional flint stone cottage pub blends seamlessly into the surrounding Bloomsbury countryside. Obtaining its name from the local residents who would once have formed the backbone of the village team and been the pub's main clientele, the pub is now most frequented by walkers who drop in from the South Downs Way or the nearby Long Man of Wilmington.

Outside there are scented gardens full of colourful flowers and, inside, its cottage-like rooms contain two log fires in small brick fireplaces as well as attractive cricketing pastels and beams hung with cricket bats. The Cricketers offers steaks and beef from Lewes, fish from Newhaven and sausages from Seaford, and a particular highlight is the Steak and Harveys Ale Pie.

For more information see www.cricketersberwick.co.uk or call 01323 870 469.

THE WALK

LENGTH: 4.25 MILES

Taking in the ancient downland hamlets of Berwick and Alciston, this straightforward walk is divided between rolling farmland at the foot of the South Downs and a short stretch along the South Downs Way, from which there are unparalleled views over the Cuckmere Valley and the Weald.

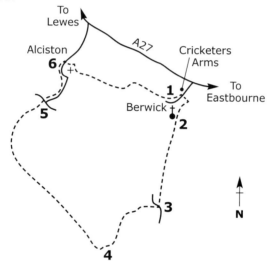

- **OS MAP:**
Explorer 123: Eastbourne & Beachy Head.

- **START POINT:**
The Cricketers Arms (BN26 6SP; grid ref TQ 519053).

- **GETTING THERE:**
Via A27 about 5 miles west of Polegate. There is ample off-street parking opposite the pub.

- **PUBLIC TRANSPORT:**
Berwick railway station is located a mile to the north of The Cricketers Arms. The Cuckmere Community Bus calls at the pub on request on certain days of the week.

1. Leaving The Cricketers Arms, cross over the road and take a gravel track through the grassy car park directly opposite, soon veering right around the edge of a large pond. Follow a narrow path to the right of a hedge and flint wall to emerge into a small pasture with **Berwick Church** immediately ahead. Cross over the pasture to a gap in the opposite corner to the left of the church. **Windover Hill** rises away to the left.

Berwick Church, built predominantly in the 12th century, contains an earlier well-like Saxon font, and the grassy bank of a barrow to the right of our path indicates this has been a sacred site since prehistoric times. Unusual features are the colourful murals by Bloomsbury artists Duncan Grant and Vanessa and Quentin Bell (see 'Berwick At a Glance', p30).

2. Pass to the left of the church, after which the path forks (TQ519049). Do not follow the path sharply round to the right, but take a clearly-marked path straight ahead through the centre of two large arable fields with the peak of **Firle Beacon** visible on the right.

Comp Lane byway, also known as the Old Coach Road, was once part of the main route between Lewes and Eastbourne before the introduction of the A27. The underhill road remains particularly discernible between Berwick and Firle and will be rejoined at point 5 on the walk.

Ignoring a cross track leading to a barn, continue ahead towards a cream-walled house, passing to the right of paddocks to emerge by a winding track known as **Comp Lane** (TQ517039).

3. Turn left and then almost immediately right when the byway reaches a tarmac lane. From here there are panoramic views over the route just traversed, with Berwick

Church clearly visible. On the left, the first glimpses of Alfriston can be seen. When the path splits at a three-point fork, take the middle option, winding steeply to the top of the Downs. At the top (TQ510035), take a moment to enjoy the views over the Cuckmere Valley on the left, with the route of the South Downs Way rising up Windover Hill on the other side.

In the Cuckmere Valley, the churches of Alfriston, Litlington and Lullington pinpoint the locations of these downland settlements. The last of these, directly ahead from our current position, is isolated on the hill and lays claim to being one of the smallest churches in the country, measuring just 16 feet square and seating just twenty people.

4. Turn right through a gate onto the **South Downs Way,** gently climbing uphill to gain even clearer views over the Cuckmere Valley. As the route continues westwards, the sea comes into view at both Cuckmere Haven and Seaford, with Hope Gap and Seaford Head separating the two valleys. Ignore a path on the right signposted towards Berwick and at the next junction (TQ499045), where the radio masts on **Beddingham Hill** are visible ahead and Newhaven Harbour lies away to the left, turn right to follow a sheep track to a gate with a view high above Alciston. Through the gate, a narrow track with steep sides cuts steeply down the escarpment. When this meets a gate by a road leading up to Bostal Hill (TQ498050) - near Bo Beep Chalk Pit - double back along the foot of the escarpment (the other side of the gate signposts this as Alciston 3/4 mile), soon meeting a gate on the left. Turn through this and follow a narrow sunken path between trees, re-emerging onto the Old Coach Road seen earlier.

Alciston Tithe Barn stands at 170ft long and reportedly contains over 50,000 tiles.

5. Turn right along this and then almost immediately left by a memorial seat down a

Windover Hill provides an impressive backdrop to Berwick Church.

lane signed towards Alciston. Follow the lane round a barn, the largest in the county, and then past the ruin of a medieval dovecote, both of which are the remnants of a 14th century grange once owned by Battle Abbey.

6. A footpath on the right by Alciston Church is signed 'Berwick 1 mile'. This skirts the left side of the church to a stile, over which the route turns right and then almost immediately left at a fingerpost to follow a hedge line on the left with Berwick Church visible directly ahead. At the end of the field (TQ512053), turn left and then right after a few yards along an elevated ridge across the centre of the field. This soon emerges on a surfaced farm track leading into the village where a left turn by a grass-covered mini-roundabout leads back to The Cricketers Arms.

BERWICK AT A GLANCE

Looking north towards Arlington Reservoir.

- Influenced by the frescoes of Renaissance Italy, nearby Charleston residents Vanessa Bell and Duncan Grant transformed the church at Berwick with a series of murals. Revitalizing the relationship between the Arts and the Church in the early 1940s, many of the scenes contain a Sussex backdrop; 'Nativity' is set in a barn based on one at Charleston and contains additional local colour in the form of watchful Southdown lambs and a view of Mount Caburn.

- In the 14th century, Edward III made archery practice compulsory on Sundays after church and the grooves on the inside of the tower arch of Berwick Church are thought to have been cut by the sharpening of these arrows. Many archers who went to Crecy, Poitiers and Agincourt came from Berwick.

- Artist Frank Wootton, famous for his aviation illustrations during WWII, lived in nearby Alciston for many years. Virginia Woolf is believed to have set her posthumously published novel *Between the Acts* (1941) in the village, with the English country manor of Pointz Hall likely to have been based on nearby Firle Place. The village is also allegedly the last place in the country where Good Friday skipping still takes place, often featuring local women's Morris dancing team Knots of May (see 'Through the Seasons' p9).

- Berwick's name derives from the Saxon 'Bere Wic', meaning 'barley farm'. Compare the similar origin of 'Barcombe' (Walk 2).

• • • • • • • • • •

BLACKBOYS

BLACKBOYS INN

Over 600 years old, the Blackboys Inn was built in 1389 as a farmhouse and converted to an inn in the early 18th century. The pub was used as an overnight stopping place for drivers transporting charcoal and the name 'Blackboys' is believed to derive from the colour of the boys who emerged from the nearby charcoal-burning woods.

An attractive pond complete with duck house is situated next to the Blackboys Inn and there is plenty of outside seating beneath a large chestnut tree. A varied menu uses home-grown vegetables and locally-sourced meat, fish and game. For more information see www.theblackboysinn.co.uk or call 01825 890 283.

THE WALK

LENGTH: 4.75 MILES

One of the longest outings in this collection, this walk is unusual in crossing between the southern slopes of the High Weald into the lower-lying Low Weald. The route also crosses the boundary between two river catchment areas: the first small streams encountered feed the river Uck (and ultimately river Ouse), whilst those a little to the east, beyond Hawkhurst Common Wood, feed the river Cuckmere.

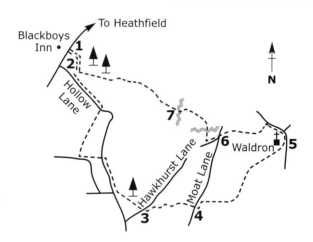

OS MAP:
Explorer 123: Eastbourne & Beachy Head

START POINT:
The Blackboys Inn (TN22 5LG; grid ref TQ522204)

GETTING THERE:
The Blackboys Inn is located on B2192 4 miles east of Uckfield and 4 miles west of Heathfield. There is a car park for patrons and some limited street parking on School Lane next to the pub.

PUBLIC TRANSPORT:
Countryliner 318 runs hourly between Uckfield and Heathfield and stops by School Lane.

1. Leave Blackboys Inn by the access road to the right of the green and cross directly over the main road (B2192) into the Woodland Trust-managed Kiln Wood, joining the route of the Vanguard Way. Head downhill, ignoring a fork, and follow signs round to the right, shortly leading down a small flight of steps and over a stream feeding the River Uck.

2. At a T-junction (TQ524201), turn right and then left through a squeeze stile onto **Hollow Lane.** When the lane bears sharply left after approximately ¼ mile, turn right by the entrance to Bushmere onto a wide enclosed grassy track. From here, the Downs stretch

Hollow Lane.

ahead as far as Windover Hill in the east. This crosses two stiles to reach **Bushbury Lane.** Turn left and when the lane bears round to the right (TQ525191), turn left onto the driveway to Peartree Cottage and then almost immediately right onto a narrow path soon leading along the right hand edge of a field. Emerging onto a lane beyond (Hollow Lane again), turn right. Opposite a junction with Beechy Road, turn through a large metal field gate and head diagonally right towards the edge of **Hawkhurst Common Wood** (TQ529186), where the way passes through a wooden gate to keep the woodland edge on the left.

3. Cross a stile onto Hawkhurst Lane, turning left and then very shortly right down a track which passes along the left hand edge of an arable field. In the field beyond (TQ533184), turn left to skirt the top edge before passing into a third field and turning right downhill to keep the hedge line on the right. A few paces to the left of the bottom corner a bridge leads over a fast flowing stream between trees (TQ535185). On the other side, follow a rough grassy path uphill to reach **Moat Lane.**

4. From here, our route diverges from that of the Vanguard Way,

Chickens by Moat Lane

turning left and then right in a few paces on an enclosed grass track, signed 'Conservation Walks'. Emerging at the top of a large sloping field (TQ540185), cross diagonally left downhill where a sign directs the path along the left hand edge of the field immediately beyond (TQ542185). Follow the path as it passes through woodland and along the left-hand edge of a field before cutting diagonally right uphill through two further fields with Waldron church up ahead. It is worth stopping at the top of the hill to enjoy spectacular views back over the Downs before passing through the churchyard into **Waldron** itself.

5. Turn left, perhaps pausing for further refreshment at Star Inn Free House, and pass through the village to the left of the war memorial. Almost immediately after the road forks, turn left onto a gravel drive beside the Memorial Hall (TQ547195) and head directly downhill to the left of rugby pitches. Veer slightly right by a tyre swing into a wood where on the left are the earthworks of a moat (TQ545193), all that remains of a medieval dwelling whose probable timber-framed structure has long since disappeared. Follow a narrow holly-lined path through the wood and cross diagonally left across a field towards a stile identifiable by a yellow marker on a high post.

6. At a lane junction on the other side, maintain direction onto **Hawkhurst Lane.** In a few yards, immediately before Fields End on the left, turn right on a partially surfaced track which leads downhill, crossing another stream before climbing briefly and emerging along the left-hand edge of a field. Follow a sign on a large tree containing an owl house and pass into woodland. At a Y-junction, fork left downhill and over another stream into Blackdown Pastures (TQ536196).

7. Maintain direction through the small pasture as the path leads back into woodland, this time on a wide grassy path with coniferous trees on the left. Continue ahead along the right-hand edge of a large field and through a wooden gate passing to the left of farm buildings to reach a concrete access drive (TQ532200). Turn left and very shortly right onto an enclosed grassy bridleway; a sign informs that this is Brownings Farm, situated on the watershed between the Ouse and Cuckmere Valleys. Immediately before reaching a wooden gate, bear right over a stile to walk along the left-hand edge of the field beyond, at the end of which a sign welcomes us back into **Kiln Wood.** Follow the path through the wood until reaching a signed junction shortly before a gate. This is point 2 on the walk and a right turn allows us to retrace our steps back to the start.

View south from Waldron church

BLACKBOYS AT A GLANCE

- The majority of charcoal sourced near Blackboys was used by the nearby Buxted iron foundry where many believe the first iron cannon in England was made in 1543. The business stopped in the early nineteenth century when the iron industry moved north to the larger deposits of coal.

- Notorious John 'Mad Jack' Fuller, born in 1757, was christened in the church in Waldron. He was later responsible for financing the building of Belle Tout lighthouse at Beachy Head, purchasing Bodiam Castle at an auction to save it from destruction and famously building a number of follies, including the sugar loaf and obelisk near Burwash - the latter known locally as the Brightling Needle.

- Part of the route passes along a carriage-driving toll ride route, established by Toll Rides (Off-road) Trust, whose aim is to allow riders to avoid dangerous stretches of road and provide enjoyable riding in areas where public access for horses is limited. For a membership fee, the majority of which goes to farmers and landowners, riders can cross agreed tracks and headlands. See www.tollrides.org.uk for more information.

• • • • • • • • • •

Looking towards Waldron Church.

WALK 5   BOREHAM STREET

BULL'S HEAD

This weather-boarded building has been a hostelry since the agricultural revolution in the early 18th Century. Once a coaching inn, The Bull's Head was the first pub Harveys bought when it became a limited company in the 1920s and its cosy wood-panelled interior is lined with illustrations of the pub through the ages. In early 2009 it became the subject of a BBC article when it very nearly suffered the fate of many rural pubs, but landlord Mike Corfield, formerly of the popular Elephant and Castle in Lewes, stepped in to prevent its closure.

The pub is attached to eight acres of land which are used to aid revenue in the form of clay pigeon shoots or car boot sales. Potatoes, eggs and pork cultivated on the land are used in the pub kitchen, and Sussex beef 'Bull Burgers', Hastings fish and Sunday roasts are particular menu highlights. Regular events include live music and quiz nights.

For more information see www.bullsheadborehamstreet.co.uk or call 01323 831 981.

THE WALK

LENGTH: 4 MILES

Herstmonceux Castle and Observatory form a focal point to much of this pleasant walk and there are clear views to be had of both. The route passes along quiet lanes and through small woodland, initially following the historic 1066 Country Trail. Just before Herstmonceux Place is the opportunity to look westwards across Pevensey Levels to where the South Downs rise at Eastbourne.

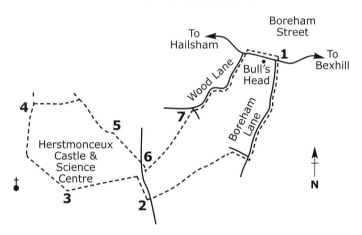

OS MAP:
Explorer 124: Hastings & Bexhill

START POINT:
The Bull's Head (BN27 4SG; TQ666113)

GETTING THERE:
Via A271 about 6 miles east of Hailsham. There is no alternative parking in Boreham Street itself but there is a large lay-by near Herstmonceux Castle (BN27 1RN; TQ653104). This is point 2 on the walk

PUBLIC TRANSPORT:
Stagecoach bus service 98 runs Mon - Sat from Eastbourne, Hailsham and Bexhill

1. Leaving the pub, turn right down a road signed 'Boreham Lane Narrow Road'. After roughly half a mile, turn right onto Jenners Lane. Head downhill and after a few yards turn left into a large field, joining the **1066 Country Walk** to skirt the field's right-hand edge. In the far corner, a signpost leads the path onto a small wooded ridge. Maintain direction, crossing a stream. Over a stile, follow the left-hand edge of the field beyond, from which it is possible to glimpse the distinctive green copper oxide domes of Herstmonceux Science Centre to the right. The path leads to a road opposite a sign that reads 'Herstmonceux Castle 300 yards' (TQ654101).

Wealden cattle seen from the 1066 Country Walk, which runs from Pevensey Castle via Battle Abbey to Rye and retraces the approximate footsteps of William the Conqueror when he invaded Saxon Britain.

2. Turn right and, carefully following the verge on the left-hand side of the road, take a footpath on the left immediately before the entrance road to the castle itself, signed '**Herstmonceux Church** ³/₄ mile'. (Walkers who choose to start the outing from the lay-by at TQ653104 will join the route here). The path runs along the edge of woodland by the south boundary of Herstmonceux Science Centre. Maintain direction steadily downhill, soon glimpsing the turrets of Herstmonceux Castle away to the right and the ridge of the Downs ahead. At the bottom of the hill, head through a metal gate to emerge into a large field. Continue ahead to a finger post in the centre of the field (TQ646102). A detour straight ahead at this point leads to Herstmonceux Church itself, from which there is an outstanding panorama to the west.

Herstmonceux Castle.

3. Turn right at the fingerpost and follow the path to a stile in the corner. Crossing this, turn left onto a narrow enclosed path between fences and over a surfaced drive into a field. The brick-built Tudor castle is now clearly visible. Head directly ahead uphill into a small woodland. After a few yards, meet a cross path (TQ643105) and turn right on a signed bridleway. Follow the bridleway through a metal gate out of the woodland and downhill into a valley. To the left, the easterly extent of the South Downs can be seen whilst ahead is **Herstmonceux Place.**

4. In the bottom of the valley, join a track and after 50 yards turn right through a metal gate (TQ645110) and cross directly ahead, following the line of the valley, to a gate in the opposite boundary (TQ648110). With a barn and two houses visible to the left, turn right through the gate and continue ahead through woodland, descending gradually downhill and passing a small pond on the left. A building glimpsed on the right is the back of a 1930s folly situated in the parkland surrounding Herstmonceux Castle.

Looking back towards Herstmonceux Place.

5. On meeting a footpath junction a few yards beyond the folly, bear right to head uphill through woodland, following a boundary fence on the right-hand boundary. Cross a stile at the top of the wood to emerge in the corner of a field with the Science Centre immediately on the right. Head diagonally across the field to the far opposite corner where the path leads through a metal gate on the left to rejoin the main road (TQ653104).

6. Turn right for 50 yards and cross the road immediately opposite the entrance road to Herstmonceux Castle, heading northeast through woodland (carpeted with bluebells and wood anemonies in spring) on a clear path which soon passes to the right of a pond. On meeting a T-junction just after this, turn left and follow a signed path gradually uphill and eventually emerge over a stile onto a country lane.

7. Turn left and then almost immediately right onto **Wood Lane.** Follow this as it winds northward to emerge on the main road through Boreham Street. Cross this and turn right to follow the footway back to The Bull's Head.

View northwards over the High Weald from the road into Boreham Street.

BOREHAM STREET AT A GLANCE

- Boreham Street is one of a line of small villages situated on a ridge which marks the southern boundary of the High Weald. The name 'Boreham' is itself possibly derived from the Anglo Saxon 'Beorgh Hamme' (the village on the hill).

- In 1957 the Royal Greenwich Observatory moved from London to Herstmonceux Castle grounds where there was less light pollution. In 1988 the observatory moved to Cambridge, but the observatory now exists as a visitor attraction. The site itself is actually a few degrees east of the meridian line, which can be found in Lewes (see Walk 13).

- Herstmonceux Castle itself is one of the oldest significant brick buildings still standing in England. Constructed in a lake which acts as a large moat, the castle was predominantly designed with grandeur, rather than defence, in mind. Today it is the home of the Bader International Study Centre of Queen's University, Canada, but the Elizabethan gardens and parkland are open to the public. For more information and opening times see www.herstmonceux-castle.com

- In the 1820s, Thomas Smith of Herstmonceux created the Sussex Trug, an invention that would have a profound effect on gardeners worldwide. In 1851, he attended The Great Exhibition held in The Crystal Palace in London and Queen Victoria personally ordered some as gifts for members of the Royal Family.

•••••••••

WALK 6

BRIGHTON

LORD NELSON

No collection of walks in Sussex would be complete without mention of Brighton and The Lord Nelson is the perfect place to start an exploration of this historic city. Situated but a few yards away from the station itself, The Lord Nelson is always a hive of activity, with regular live music and weekly quiz nights.

Inside, there are two small but comfortable saloon bars, with a conservatory for warmer days and a log fire for those less so. Free Wi-Fi and an extensive range of real ale, cider, lager and quality new world wines are on offer. For more information see www.thelordnelsoninn.co.uk or call 01273 695 872.

THE WALK

LENGTH: 2 MILES

This short stroll gives a brief insight into some of the most iconic areas of the city, meandering through the North Laine and twittens of The Lanes to reach the seafront, before turning back through a succession of lawns past the Royal Pavilion.

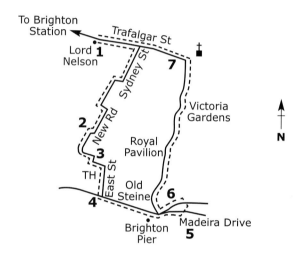

OS MAP:
Explorer 122: Brighton & Hove

START POINT:
The Lord Nelson Inn (BN1 4ED; grid ref TQ312048)

GETTING THERE:
The Lord Nelson does not have its own car park and there is very limited street parking in Brighton. The nearest multi-storey car parks are at Whitecross Street (BN1 4FE) and New England Street (BN1 4GN).

PUBLIC TRANSPORT:
Brighton Station is 200 yards from The Lord Nelson Inn and is well served by rail and bus services from across the county.

1. Turn right and then right again after 150 yards onto Sydney Street. This section of the walk passes through the centre of the **North Laine,** a quirky area full of unusual independent shops and, in summer, street art and music. Our route turns right at the end of Sydney Street and then almost immediately left onto the narrow Kensington Gardens. Continue ahead onto Gardner Street, passing the Komedia, which has won Chortle's Best Comedy Venue in the South a record-breaking seven times. At the end of this, turn left and then right onto New Road, a recently re-developed street by the Theatre Royal and Pavilion Theatres running behind the Royal Pavilion, which will be visited later.

2. From New Road, turn right and then left over a pedestrian crossing onto Meeting House Lane to enter the maze of small alleyways or 'twittens' which make up **The Lanes.** Once the heart of the original fishing settlement of Brighthelmstone, The Lanes are now a popular tourist shopping area

A bustling Kensington Gardens in North Laine.

comprising many specialist boutiques and jewellers' shops. Passing Riddle & Finns champagne and oyster bar and Sweet Williams Fudge Shop, our way continues directly ahead, following the twitten round

to the left after the Bath Arms. Continue ahead through Brighton Square, emerging onto the larger plaza of Brighton Place.

3. Turn right then left to pass by the side of The Sussex to reach East Street, once the easterly boundary of the original fishing settlement and the town's slum, but now home to many expensive shops and bars. Turn right towards the sea, with the **Town Hall** soon glimpsed on the right. Film buffs will recognise the road as the location of the culmination of the riots in the

1960s film Quadrophenia and indeed an alleyway on the right by 11 East Street is known as **Quadrophenia Alley.**

Brighton Town Hall, built in 1830-2.

Quadrophenia Alley.

4. Emerging by the seafront, cross over onto the promenade itself with the skeletal structure of the West Pier visible off to the right and the Palace Pier, now known simply as **Brighton Pier,** almost directly ahead.

Brighton has had a pier since 1823 in the form of the Chain Pier, subject of a painting by Constable and once a landing stage for ships from Dieppe, but was eventually destroyed by a storm in 1896. Today, Brighton Pier is the only pier open to the public and its iconic edifice has featured in popular culture from Graham Greene's Brighton Rock to Carry On at Your Convenience.

Turn left and soon pass the entrance to Brighton Pier, perhaps taking a moment to explore the pier itself, and continue along **Madeira Drive,** a wide road built on reclaimed land whose function is to protect the cliff face from coastal erosion. Throughout the year, Madeira Drive is often used as the finish line for many events such as the London to Brighton Bike Ride and Veteran Car Run.

5. Just past the Aquarium Station of the **Volks Railway** (the world's oldest operating electric railway, built in 1883 by Magnus Volk and running almost to the present site of Brighton Marina) cross the road and up a wide sloping green-railed path which doubles back and then up steps to reach the main seafront road. From here there are good views over both piers and Royal Albion Hotel, once the site of the house of Dr Richard Russell, a renowned physician who popularised the use of seawater for a variety of maladies in the 1750s.

6. Cross the road immediately before reaching Brighton Aquarium and maintain direction, aiming towards a large park. Cross through the centre of this by a large fountain to reach a war memorial. This area is **Old Steine,** once used by fishermen to mend boats. Beneath the lawns a stream is buried in huge Victorian sewers. Follow the road to the left of the war memorial, skirting the edge of the **Royal Pavilion,** the exotic dwelling designed predominantly by John Nash and built for George, Prince Regent (and later King George IV) at the turn of the 19th century. Immediately after passing a statue of

Madeira Drive.

Old Steine.

George IV himself, follow two further parks which would once have been fashionable promenades at the height of the Regency period.

7. At the entrance to the imposing structure of **St Peter's Church,** Brighton's parish church, turn left up Trafalgar Street where The Lord Nelson can be found a few hundred yards away on the left.

The Royal Pavilion.

BURWASH

ROSE & CROWN

Once an Elizabethan coaching inn, the timber-framed building of the Rose & Crown was refaced in the 18th century with painted brick on the ground floor and tile-hung above. A Grade II listed building, low beams and a glass-covered well greet visitors into the restaurant and bar area, whilst outside is a covered courtyard and partially decked garden area. Two large inglenook fireplaces with log burning stoves are also particularly welcoming on those colder days.

Food is served both lunchtime and evening, with main courses including delicious Harveys beer-battered fish and chips and half shoulder of lamb braised in rosemary and sage. The Rose & Crown also has four letting rooms all with en suite shower rooms. For more information see www.roseandcrown-burwash.co.uk or call 01435 882 600.

THE WALK

LENGTH: 5 MILES

Burwash is situated on a ridge between two valleys and this walk explores both the Rother valley to the north and the Dudwell valley to the south, with both rivers clearly visible. On the latter part of the journey the route passes by the luxurious mansion of Batemans, one-time residence of Rudyard Kipling.

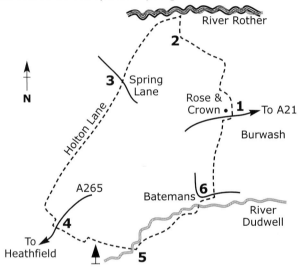

- **OS MAP:**
  Explorer 136: High Weald

- **START POINT:**
  The Rose & Crown (TN19 7ER; grid ref TQ675248)

- **GETTING THERE:**
  Via A265 six miles east of Heathfield. There is a free car park at the centre of Burwash (grid ref. TQ673247).

- **PUBLIC TRANSPORT:**
  Renown coach service 318/9 runs Mon-Sat between Uckfield and Etchingham. Etchingham rail station is 3 miles from Burwash and located on the London-Hastings line.

1. Continue along the track **(Ham Lane)** beside the Rose & Crown, which heads downhill between fields. When the track bends towards an isolated house onto a driveway marked as no public right of way (TQ673254), cross a stile on the left and then a second a few paces beyond. Head directly right across a sloping field towards **Honeybrook Wood,** entering this by a stile in the bottom right corner. Turn right into the wood, following the path between trees and emerging onto a bridge over a small stream. Turn right again and cut across the corner of a field and over another bridge immediately beside a field gate.

2. Walk along the left-hand edge of a large field beside the small stream of **Seller's Brook** and turn left through a wide gap halfway along the boundary (TQ669259). Keep along the left-hand edge and at the top corner maintain direction through a gate onto a track climbing gradually uphill. Pass tennis courts in the grounds of Franchise Manor and a few paces before the end of a field, cross a stile on the right to join the drive leading from the manor. Turn left along the drive to reach **Spring Lane** (TQ662253).

3. Bear left onto Spring Lane and then turn right in a few paces onto a narrow bridleway which soon becomes a hedge-lined track known as **Holton Lane.** This track, often muddy even in summer, leads through trees along a ridge with views over the High Weald to the right. After just over a mile this finally descends through a wood, passing to the right of

Looking towards the rooftops of Burwash on the skyline. Just beyond this is an apple orchard by Mottynsden Farm, whilst behind is the Rother valley, often prone to flooding.

a cream-walled house. When the track forks immediately below a metal barn, take the left branch to emerge via Lower Bough Farm onto the A265 just outside Burwash Weald (TQ654233).

4. Turn right and then almost immediately left onto a driveway by **Weald House.** When the driveway ends, continue directly ahead along the left-hand side of the converted oast house of Pear Tree Cottage and pass through a metal gate into a small field. Maintain direction and, halfway along the left-hand boundary, cross a stile to follow the right-hand edge of the field beyond towards a gate in the bottom corner. Through the gate, keep along the left-hand edge of a large field and turn right immediately before another gate in the corner (TQ658232) to head down a slope and into woodland via a kissing gate. The path winds through **Bog Wood** with the river Dudwell, much smaller than its counterpart in the Rother valley, soon visible through the trees. On leaving the wood, keep ahead along the bottom edge of a meadow and soon cross a bridge over the river into the field on the right.

5. Bear left and continue ahead to pass through the right-hand of two gates on the far side of the field. Follow a line of trees along the left-hand boundary of the field beyond and then veer left through a

Kipling's home at Bateman's, now owned by the National Trust. His study remains much as he left it, reflecting his oriental tastes, and his 1928 Rolls Royce Phantom is on display in the garage.

View over the Dudwell valley.

large gap into the adjacent field, bearing right soon to rejoin the river Dudwell. Keep ahead, ignoring a path forking left, with the grand mansion of Bateman's soon visible. The path follows a stream on the right towards a pond, passing to the left-hand side of this and then left again just before a weatherboarded mill to reach a drive. Bear left along the drive to arrive at **Bateman's** itself (TQ671238).

6. By the original entrance to Bateman's, turn right along a lane for 200 yards and then cross a stile on the left (TQ673238). Head up the right-hand edge of a field, passing into the field beyond and round the edge of a small woodland. Looking behind, there are fine views back over the Dudwell valley and an obelisk, the **Brightling Needle,** can be spied on the horizon (see Burwash at a Glance). The path leads alongside hedges and through a meadow before reaching a footpath junction in the final sloping field just below Burwash. Bear diagonally right uphill, crossing a stile to the left of a white house and onto a narrow enclosed path which emerges on Burwash High Street. Turn right and then left in a few paces by a sign leading back to the Rose & Crown.

BURWASH AT A GLANCE

- Bateman's was home to Rudyard Kipling, writer of *The Jungle Books* and the poem *'If'*. Moving from his house in Rottingdean in 1902, he remained at Bateman's until his death in 1936. The house, a Jacobean mansion built for a Wealden ironmaster from local sandstone, is now owned by the National Trust and is open to the public from Easter to October, Sat-Weds (Tel: 01435 882302). The local area surrounding Bateman's features in many of Kipling's short stories and poems, particularly in *Puck of Pook's Hill* and *Rewards and Fairies.*

- Burwash was once a prosperous centre of the Wealden iron industry, but later became, like many places along the South Coast, a notorious smuggling town. Today, many attractive listed buildings line the High Street, mainly dating from the 17th and 18th Century.

- Brightling Needle, situated to the south of Burwash in Brightling Park, was one of many follies erected by John 'Mad Jack' Fuller. Built in the early 19th century and probably designed by Sir Robert Smirke, who erected other buildings in the parish for Fuller at the same time, the Brightling Needle is one of the highest points in Sussex, standing at over 645ft above sea level.

· · · · · · · · · ·

River Dudwell.

EASTBOURNE

LAMB

Situated adjacent to the Church of St Mary in Eastbourne's Old Town, this Grade II listed building is one of the oldest pubs in England. As well as posessing half-timbering dating from the 16th century, the vaulted medieval cellar is probably contemporaneous with the church itself and dates back to the 12th century. The inn is said to be connected by a subterraneous passage with the Old Parsonage, part of which has been traced and uncovered.

Like the church adjacent, the pub sits on the slope of the Bourne stream which gives the town its name. As a result of increased development, the stream passes mostly underground today, but traces still can be seen in nearby Motcombe Gardens.

The large room on the first floor of The Lamb was known as the ball-room and for many years was the only assembly room in the town where auctions and public meetings could be held. Today the pub is one of many Harveys pubs to feature in the CAMRA Good Beer Guide.

THE WALK

LENGTH: 3.75/5 MILES

A walk which takes in all the elements which define Eastbourne's character, the route begins in the original heart of the town before heading towards the sea and along the esplanade with views of the Martello Wish Tower and Victorian pier. After this there is the option either to walk through the charming parish of Meads or detour over the South Downs, with vistas over Eastbourne Level towards Hastings.

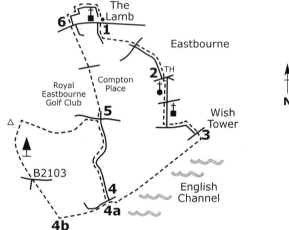

● **OS MAP:**
● Explorer 123: Eastbourne & Beachy Head

● **START POINT:**
● The Lamb Inn (BN21 1HH; grid ref TV599995)

● **GETTING THERE:**
● The Lamb is situated in Old Town on the A259 into Eastbourne.
● The pub does not have its own car park but there is limited street
● parking nearby

● **PUBLIC TRANSPORT:**
● Brighton & Hove bus service 12 from Eastbourne, Seaford and
● Brighton stops virtually outside The Lamb. Eastbourne railway
● station is just under 3/4 mile to the southeast along the same road

1. Cross immediately opposite the pub onto **Borough Lane,** where a plaque on **Pilgrims** house to the right informs that Charles Dickens made several visits here during the 1830s. Follow the flint wall of Manor Gardens and, on reaching the green gates of Lockwood, turn left onto a path which skirts the right-hand edge of **Gildredge Park.** When the path forks, take the left-hand option and then continue directly ahead onto a road leading into the park (Saffrons Road). Maintain direction, signposted towards the Town Hall.

2. When Saffrons Road ends by the Town Hall itself, turn left and then almost immediately right beside a Roman Catholic Church on Grange Road. Follow the road past the imposing edifice of **Eastbourne College** and a further church and, at the end, turn left onto Silverdale Road; The Grand Hotel, affectionately known as 'The White Palace' is visible directly ahead. As the road bears left, turn right past The Grand Hotel and cross directly over King Edward's Parade into **Western Lawns** (TV612980).

Eastbourne Town Hall.

In Western Lawns stands a statue of William Cavendish, 7th Duke of Devonshire, who was responsible for the majority of Eastbourne's development in the mid-19th century. Beyond is the 'Wish Tower', originally built as one of a chain along the south coast of England to counter an invasion threat from Napoleon.

3. Passing through Western Lawns, turn right along a broad seafront esplanade. A few yards to the left is the start of the **Wealdway.** This part of our walk is a very leisurely stroll of approximately ³/₄ mile which looks ahead towards cliffs near Beachy Head, whilst behind the coastline stretches out as far as Hastings. Just beyond a series of beach chalets, the path heads uphill on Holywell Drive, passing Holywell Retreat, a public garden located on the site of a disused chalk pit. At the top of the hill, turn left around the right-hand edge of Helen Gardens, emerging onto the seafront road opposite Holywell Road (TV601972). From here there are two options, depending on stamina, time constraints and weather.

4. For the shorter and less strenuous option, cross over onto Holywell Road, which soon merges into **Meads Street** to pass through the affluent Meads village. A row of houses between 22-28 Meads Street was completely destroyed by an air raid in March 1943, a sobering reminder that Eastbourne was the most bombed town in Sussex during WWII. At a T-junction by the Parish Hall, turn right onto Meads Road and take the first left onto Gaudick Road; shortly before this, the church of St John can be seen - set ablaze by the first air raid on Eastbourne on 4 May 1942 but today remaining a thriving heart of the parish. Continue ahead on Gaudick Road, maintaining direction over a road junction to rejoin the longer route at point 5.

4a. For the longer route, which is most worthwhile on a clear day, continue ahead towards the start of the **South Downs Way.** When the main road shortly bears right, maintain direction, signed Beachy Head 1¹/₄ mile. This is initially a very steep ascent, but a kiosk at the foot of the hill allows for refuelling and the view back over Eastbourne as the path climbs makes for ample excuse to pause. At a finger post,

fork right away from the South Downs Way (which continues to Beachy Head), and rejoin the Wealdway.

4b. At the summit (TV594969) another fingerpost guides right onto a cross track, signed to Willingdon and

Jevington. Maintain direction, keeping to the left of a further fingerpost and crossing a wide grassy track to reach a road junction (TV590975). Cross the road carefully and continue to follow the signed bridleway to Jevington, skirting to the left of woodland. On reaching a cross path, turn right on a signed path towards **Paradise Drive,** skirting to the right of a pond by a trig point where a seat encourages a brief pause. Join a grassy track heading SE downhill (TV589982), skirting to the right of woodland and emerging on Paradise Drive at the bottom of the hill (TV598982). This is the start of the bridleway section of the South Downs Way: a sign here reads 'Winchester 100 miles'. Turn right to follow Paradise Drive downhill and turn left after 175 yards onto **Gaudick Road.**

5. At the end of Gaudick Road, go through a metal kissing gate and head directly downhill across a golf course, following fingerposts and keeping both a distant church and a nearer clubhouse on the left. Shortly, the Town Hall and Compton Place, often visited by King Edward VII and one of only three Grade I listed buildings in Eastbourne, can be seen on the right. On the far side, descend through a small strip of woodland to re-emerge onto Paradise Drive (TV599989). Cross this and descend steps to the right of a memorial gateway to reach a wide walled path which eventually emerges via a gravel track onto Glebe Close. Turn right, almost immediately joining Vicarage Road and maintaining direction downhill, passing Vicarage Drive to emerge onto the A259.

6. Cross this by the pedestrian crossing and head down Green Street, from which there is a view ahead to the western spur of Cold Crouch Hill above Willingdon. Take the second right onto Greenfield Road, turning right at the end onto Parsonage Road and, immediately before a white brick house, turn left down a narrow walled path into Motcombe Gardens. Here, the 'bourne' or river which gave the original Anglo-Saxon settlement its name rises in a small pond in the valley.

On the far side of Motcombe Gardens turn right onto Motcombe Lane, where a silhouette on the brickwork at No. 7 marks where comedian and magician Tommy Cooper lived from 1921-1984. In a few yards, turn right up Lawns Avenue and then right again up Ocklynge Road, passing the entrance drive to the 16th century Old Parsonage and adjacent Old Parsonage Barn, to emerge by the side of The Lamb.

EASTBOURNE AT A GLANCE

- Britain's first motor omnibus service started in Eastbourne in 1903, making the town the first municipal operator of motor buses in the world.

- Eastbourne can claim some notable regular visitors. Karl Marx and Frederick Engels were often in the area; the latter's ashes were scattered from Beachy Head at his request. In 1905 French composer Claude Debussy (1862-1918) completed his symphony 'La Mer' while staying at The Grand Hotel, which has also been graced by such prominent figures as Winston Churchill, Charlie Chaplin and Elgar.

- Theatrical life in Eastbourne was enhanced with the opening of the Royal Hippodrome Theatre (originally the Theatre Royal) in Seaside Road, in 1883, Its architect, C.J. Phipps, was also responsible for the Lyric, Queen Hall and Savoy Theatres in London.

- The author George Orwell spent the years from 1911 to 1916 at boarding school in Eastbourne and is believed to have taken inspiration for the farm in Animal Farm from 'Chalk Farm' in Willingdon, a village that forms part of the conurbation that makes up Eastbourne.

• • • • • • • • • •

Motcombe Gardens.

EAST GRINSTEAD

OLD MILL

Originally known as Dunnings Mill after a one-time landowner, this former flour mill is recorded in documents as far back as 1713, but is thought to be much older. Although the mill was demolished in the early 20th century, a small stream still passes beneath where the mill once stood via an attractive working replica of the old water wheel.

Containing a decked area over the stream complete with patio heaters, The Old Mill is popular with many. Taken over by Whiting & Hammond in 2005, who also own pubs in Tonbridge, Langney and Mark Cross, there is even breakfast served on Saturdays and Sundays for those who fancy an early start. For more information see www.theolddunningsmill.co.uk or call 01342 326 341.

THE WALK

LENGTH: 4 MILES

This gentle outing passes through the undulating fields and woodland of the High Weald towards Weir Wood Reservoir, which was formed by damming the river Medway. The route follows the Sussex Border Path alongside the reservoir before ascending by the attractive country house of Standen and following a section of the High Weald Landscape Trail back to The Old Mill.

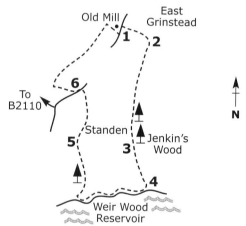

OS MAP:
Explorer 135: Ashdown Forest

START POINT:
The Old Mill (RH19 4AT; grid ref TQ392369)

GETTING THERE:
Via A22 or B2110 on West Hoathly Road to the south of East Grinstead. There is limited on-street parking opposite the pub

PUBLIC TRANSPORT:
Metrobus service 84 between Crawley and East Grinstead centre stops outside The Old Mill. East Grinstead railway station is just over a mile to the north and East Grinstead itself is well served by buses from around the county.

1. Outside The Old Mill, turn right onto Dunning's Road and then almost immediately left into Sunnyside Recreation Ground, soon heading into woodland to walk beside a small stream. When the path forks, take the right-hand option and closely follow the woodland's right-hand edge. At a signed junction a few yards later (TQ395366), turn right through a wooden gate out of the woodland into a field, taking the right-hand option again towards a gate in the opposite boundary.

2. Head uphill alongside the left-hand edge of the sloping field beyond, passing a small concealed pond. Follow a clearly marked path ahead through a strip of fenced woodland before keeping along the left-hand edge of the adjacent field beside **Rushett's Shaw.** In the far left corner, head through a gate into **Jenkin's Wood,** almost immediately descending to cross a stream.

3. On emerging from the woodland, cross a stile at a footpath junction and continue directly ahead over a small field towards a metal kissing gate halfway along the opposite boundary. Head through a patch of light woodland to reach a stile in the corner of a field with the ridge of Ashdown Forest now in view on the horizon and **Weir Wood Reservoir** just visible ahead. Follow the right-hand edge of the field, ignoring a turning on the right, and head over a stile in the far corner marked by a High Weald Circular Walk sign. This leads directly into two gently sloping fields and through a gap between hedgerows to reach Weir Wood Reservoir itself.

Weir Wood Reservoir was formed by damming the River Medway in 1954.

Weir Wood Reservoir.

Primarily used as a source of the South East's water supply, a variety of watersports are practised on the reservoir and the western end is a local nature reserve and SSSI, home to great crested grebe and migrating osprey. Just before turning away from the reservoir it is possible to discern an old road which was flooded to make way for the reservoir.

4. On meeting the reservoir and joining the **Sussex Border Path** (TQ398352), turn right, following the contours of the water's edge, passing an information board for Standen Rocks, sandstone outcrops in the hillside. On reaching a second information board, turn right by a signed stile (TQ387349) and climb a well-trodden path to the left of telegraph poles to pass one such sandstone outcrop before heading into fern-covered woodland. Continue up a steep slope, curving to the left to meet a Y-junction and taking the right fork over a stile to climb through the edge of a woodland, carpeted with bluebells in spring.

View towards Ashdown Forest.

5. Emerging at a footpath junction, take the opportunity to look back over Weir Wood Reservoir and the High Weald before continuing uphill, following the High Weald Landscape Trail alongside the right-hand of a field with the National Trust property of **Standen** to the right.

Both a showpiece of the Arts & Crafts movement and a spectacular example of the 1890's country house, Standen was designed by architect Philip Webb and decorated inside with William Morris fabrics, carpets and wallpapers. Now owned by the National Trust, it is open to the public from Easter until the end of October, Weds-Sun, plus Mondays in August (Tel: 01342 323029)

At the top of the field, follow the path around the perimeter of Standen to reveal a view over **Saint Hill House** and a glimpse of the North Downs to the left. Continue ahead to reach a drive leading to Standen and bear left shortly to reach West Hoathly Road (TQ388361).

6. Turn left and almost immediately right into woodland, signposted **High Weald Landscape Trail** and Standen Trail. At a Y-junction, take the left fork

The grandiose 18th century manor of Saint Hill House was bought by Scientology's founder and science fiction writer L. Ron Hubbard in 1959 and was the religion's world headquarters throughout the 1960s and 1970s; it remains the headquarters of the Church of Scientology in the UK today.

to walk alongside the right-hand edge of large playing fields. Halfway along the right-hand edge, take a signposted right turning (TQ384361) which follows the Landscape Trail through a mixture of woodland and rough grassland to emerge eventually onto a small lane (Medway Drive). At the end of this, turn right for 100 yards to return to West Hoathly Road (TQ391367), with The Old Mill a few yards away on the left.

EAST GRINSTEAD AT A GLANCE

- Already a bustling market town by the Middle Ages, East Grinstead has held a market charter since 1221. Today, the High Street contains the longest continuous run of 14th-century timber-framed buildings in England.

- During the Second World War, the town was a secondary target for German bombers who failed to make their primary target in London. During the evening of 9 July 1943, a German bomb fell on the Whitehall Cinema in the High Street. 108 people were killed, the largest loss of life of any single air raid in Sussex.

- John Mason Neale, who wrote the popular Christmas Carol *Good King Wenceslas* in the early 19th century, was once warden of East Grinstead's Sackville College, a sandstone almshouse built in 1609.

- Sir Patrick Moore, Neil Gaiman, Jane Leeves and Louise Redknapp have all also lived in the town.

- The Bluebell Railway operates a preserved heritage steam railway along a nine-mile stretch of the Lewes-East Grinstead line between Kingscote (two miles south of East Grinstead) and Sheffield Park. Many filming shoots take place on the railway, including The Railway Children (2000). At present Metrobus service 473 links East Grinstead station to Kingscote, although the Bluebell Railway will soon be connected to the town.
  For more information see www.bluebell-railway.co.uk

• • • • • • • • • •

East Grinstead High Street.

EAST HOATHLY

FORESTERS ARMS

It is widely believed that the name of 'Hoathly' derives from the Saxon 'hath leah', meaning a heather-covered clearing amid the trees, and the Foresters Arms takes its name from the forestry and woodworking industries that would once have been prevalent in the area. Even in the mid-19th century a number of wood sellers, carpenters, joiners and timber hewers are still recorded among the large proportion of farm labourers.

Over three centuries old, the pub was once on the main road from Eastbourne to London and only since 1992 has the A22 bypassed the peaceful village. There is attractive panelling and bay windows in the dining area and one bar ceiling is covered with sheet music from the 1940s and 1950s.

For more information call 01825 840208

THE WALK

LENGTH: 3.5 MILES

This short stroll takes in several points of interest as it passes through the gently undulating fields of the sparsely populated Low Weald. Due to the relatively high elevation of the area the walk also offers particularly expansive views southwards towards the line of the South Downs.

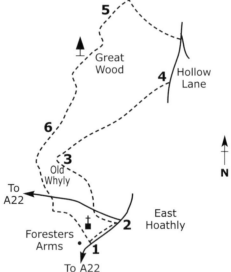

- **OS MAP:**
  Explorer 123: Eastbourne & Beachy Head

- **START POINT:**
  The Foresters Arms (BN8 6DF; grid ref TQ521161)

- **GETTING THERE:**
  Via A22 about five miles southeast of Uckfield. There is ample parking in the village and a car park next to the church.

- **PUBLIC TRANSPORT:**
  Stagecoach bus service 54 runs between Eastbourne and Uckfield Mon-Sat.

1. Turn left from the Foresters Arms and follow South Street into the centre of East Hoathly. A plaque on the left marks the residence of Thomas Turner, a mid-18th century village shopkeeper whose detailed diaries provide an intriguing insight into everyday life in pre-industrial England.

2. Bear round to the left by East Hoathly Village Stores. Shortly after passing tennis courts on the left, cross the road and turn right through a squeeze gate into a field (TQ521164), known locally as the 'Searchlight' field as a searchlight battery was located here during WWII, trained to pinpoint and illuminate enemy aircraft at night. Head diagonally left and, over another squeeze gate, turn left on a track. Maintain direction as the track winds round to the left and skirt round the edge of a paddock into light woodland of cherry trees. Continue straight ahead as the path crosses a stream and through the centre of a grass field to the right of the grand Georgian manor house of **Old Whyly.** It is thought by many that the unusual name of 'Whyly' derives from the Old English Wéoh (shrine) and léah (wood or clearing), suggesting that this may once have been an ancient heathen site of worship.

One of a series of milestones on the A22 erected in the 18th century by the Turnpike Trusts. The distance is to Bow Bells Church in London and the buckle symbol is a reference to the coat of arms of the Pelham family, who once owned much land in Sussex.

3. Immediately before reaching a wooden gate leading onto a drive (TQ518168), turn right to follow the left-hand edge of the field. The way now continues along the edge of three further fields on wide grassy margins beside woodland. In the last of these, keep alongside the boundary as the margin turns easterly and makes a beeline for a white weatherboarded building. To the left of this, the path joins **Hollow Lane** (TQ528175).

4. Turn left and, immediately after a junction with Laundry Lane, turn left onto a stony track leading to **Piper's Workshops.** Follow this as it bears round to the right and, when the track ends, maintain

Looking south from the field margins above Old Whyly.

direction along the right-hand edge of a field. On meeting a footpath junction at the end, continue straight ahead to a lone tree a few paces away, from which the path bears left to a small wooden bridge in the left boundary (TQ523181). A sign on the bridge denotes that our route has now joined that of the **Wealdway,** which is followed back to the Foresters Arms.

The Wealdway is an 80-mile long-distance footpath through the Kentish and Sussex Weald beginning at Gravesend on the Thames estuary. Our route meets this on two other occasions in this collection: at Withyham and at Eastbourne, which marks the Wealdway's southernmost extent.

5. Over the bridge, maintain direction across the centre of a large field, passing to the left of a pylon. Almost immediately to the left of this, a stile leads into another field; cut across the corner of this and over a further stile into woodland which is filled with bluebells in spring. Follow the path through the centre of the wood and pass the graves of three racehorses, which include Irish Oaks winner Princess Pati. Beyond this, an enclosed path leads downhill.

From here there is a breathtaking panorama of the distant South Downs stretching from Wilmington Hill almost directly ahead to Chanctonbury Hill in the west. Radio masts pinpoint the locations of Beddingham Hill, Devil's Dyke and Truleigh Hill, the glint of cars just discernible in the west marking the site of Ditchling Beacon.

View of the South Downs. The gap in the hills denotes the Ouse Valley, with an unusual perspective on Mount Caburn to the right.

6. Maintain direction as the path joins a concrete drive by outbuildings and stables before passing through the gated entrance to **Hesmonds Stud** and onto a drive bordered by wide verges full of daffodils in spring. When this reaches a main road, cross immediately opposite to follow the left-hand boundary of a small field. At a T-junction, turn left alongside the edge of woodland which in May is filled with bluebells and nightingales. Out of sight are the remains of a moated medieval dwelling (a similar site can be seen at Blackboys: see p34). Beyond the woodland a narrow path leads uphill to emerge by a primary school and East Hoathly Parish Church, which has the rare distinction of possessing no known dedication. Keep ahead after walking through the churchyard to return to South Street and the Foresters Arms.

EAST HOATHLY AT A GLANCE

- East Hoathly village is part of the East Hoathly with Halland Parish, Halland being a smaller settlement on the other side of the A22. Together they have a population of nearly 1500. Halland is the home of the Pelham family, who produced two Prime Ministers in the 18th century: Henry Pelham (1743-54) and Thomas Pelham-Holles, Duke of Newcastle (1754-6 and 1757-62).

- Lovers of real ale can wander to the King's Head in the centre of the village to sample some of the beers by the 1648 Brewing Company, a micro-brewery based in East Hoathly since 2003. Their 'Bee-Head' beer was awarded Beer of the Festival at the 2009 South Downs Beer & Cider Festival.

- East Hoathly is the birthplace of Tony Banks, one of the founding members of prog-rock group Genesis and one of only two members (the other being bassist and guitarist Mike Rutherford) to belong to the band throughout its entire history.

- A portion of the eleven-year diary of Thomas Turner (1729-1793) is available in print, detailing his varied work for the parish, his dealings with village characters and his thoughts on literature such as Shakespeare, Laurence Sterne and Milton.

Thomas Turner's House.

GLYNDE

TREVOR ARMS

One of Harveys' first pubs, the Trevor Arms was built in 1845 in anticipation of the opening of the London, Brighton and South Coast Railway in 1865. Occupying an enviable position next to the railway and on the main coaching route from Lewes to Eastbourne, the pub remains popular owing to its proximity to Glyndebourne Opera House and Mount Caburn.

Inside, there is the opportunity to play the traditional Sussex game of toad-in-the-hole in which brass coins or 'toads' are thrown from a distance of approximately eight feet onto a lead-topped table with a hole in the middle. Despite being largely superseded by darts, many Sussex pubs have teams and the 'world championships' are held every spring in Lewes Town Hall. Other pubs offering the game of toad-in-the-hole include The Cricketers Arms at Berwick and The Swan and The Dorset Arms at Lewes.

For more information about the Trevor Arms call 01273 858 208.

THE WALK

LENGTH: 3 MILES

One of the shortest and most straightforward walks in this collection, the route begins with a short climb up to Mount Caburn, standing at 150m (480ft) above sea level. From the summit, the Ouse Valley stretches out below whilst the return journey downhill affords expansive views back over the village and towards the low-lying eastern Low Weald.

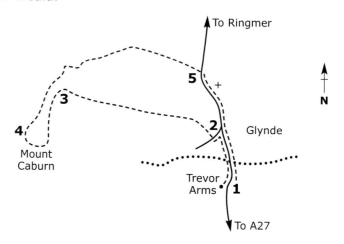

- **OS MAP:**
  Explorer 122: Brighton & Hove or Explorer 123: Eastbourne & Beachy Head

- **START POINT:**
  The Trevor Arms (BN8 6SS; grid ref TQ457086)

- **GETTING THERE:**
  About three miles southeast of Lewes via A27 or B2192 from Ringmer. A public car park can be found at TQ457088.

- **PUBLIC TRANSPORT:**
  Glynde railway station is on the main route from Eastbourne to Lewes.

1. Follow the road over the railway line and over **Glynde Reach.** Pass a small car park on the left (an alternative to the pub car park) and head through the village, noting the terraced houses once inhabited by labourers of Glynde Estates. Beyond this is the Forge, which has been in business for over 100 years and still makes iron gates and signs and undertakes metalwork repairs today.

2. Turn down **Ranscombe Lane** on the left, crossing a stile opposite the Post Office and following a track up the field. Over another stile, the path becomes steeper as it climbs its way to **Mount Caburn.** The summit is visible throughout the duration of the ascent and it is well worth pausing for a breather to take a look back over Glynde village.

Glynde village and Balcombe chalk pit. The hill directly ahead is Windover Hill, with the Cuckmere Valley hidden by the distinctive protrusion of Firle Beacon.

3. At the top of the ascent the path meets a cross track by a stile (TQ445093), from which point the northernmost tip of Lewes is just visible. Turn left, soon passing through a gate leading to **Mount Caburn Nature Reserve.** Two ditches are crossed to reach the summit, suggesting that the area was originally enclosed. Excavations have revealed evidence of Iron Age activity (c.400 BC), but archaeologists are in debate over whether the site, which contains over 140 burial pits, was a hillfort or a religious enclosure. Today, its height makes it a popular site for hang-gliding and, like much chalk downland, the area is home to adonis and chalkhill blue butterflies, as well as stonechats.

Looking south from the summit of Mount Caburn with the river Ouse snaking its way towards Newhaven.

4. Retrace the route back to the entrance to the nature reserve and return to the stile reached at point 3. Do not turn right down the path ascended earlier, but instead continue ahead for a few yards. On meeting an iron gateway on the left, turn right down a chalk track marked by a post (TQ446094). Follow the path downhill, soon passing through a copse after which there are pleasant views over the broad expanse of the low-lying eastern Low Weald, with the roofs of **Glyndebourne Opera House,** Glynde Place and Glynde Church all identifiable.

On 28 May 1934, John Christie, whose family had lived in Glyndebourne since 1617, opened Glyndebourne Opera House with a performance of Le nozze di Figaro; now it is one of the major operatic hubs in the UK with seating for 1150 people.

5. At the bottom of the hill the path emerges by **Home Farm.** Cross the road and turn right to pass Glynde Place and the unusual edifice of **Glynde Church** built in 1763-5 in Italian Renaissance style, rather than the flint constructions usually found in Sussex. After pausing to see the tomb to John Ellman, who first bred Southdown sheep in Glynde in the 1700s, follow the pavement back through the village to the Trevor Arms.

•••••••••

ISFIELD

HALFWAY HOUSE

A grade II listed building with a gabled porch, The Halfway House is situated, appropriately, halfway between the towns of Lewes and Uckfield. Partially stone-floored, inside are attractive wooden beams and low ceilings from which Harveys flagons are hung. On the walls are black and white photos of the pub exterior as it was in the early 1900s, still owned by Harveys even then. Many photos of other Harveys pubs, taken around the turn of the 20th century, also line the walls, including scenes of the Foresters Arms in East Hoathly and The Lamb Inn in Eastbourne.

A large beer garden can be found outside and there is an extensive menu which often changes for special occasions such as Burns Night and Valentines Day. Particular highlights on the dessert menu in summer have been a Baileys and white chocolate cheesecake and a delicious raspberry sorbet.

For more information call 01825 750 382.

THE WALK

LENGTH: 4.75 MILES

Similar to its Ouse valley counterpart at Barcombe, the route of this walk lies predominantly in small fields and along country lanes. At times following and crossing the river Uck, of particular interest on the journey is the Lavender Line, a small section of the Lewes-Uckfield line that has reopened as a heritage railway.

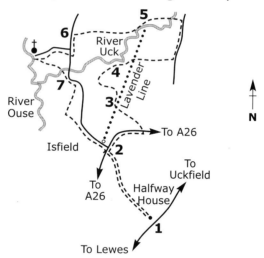

OS MAP:
Explorer 122: Brighton & Hove

START POINT:
The Halfway House (TN22 5UG; grid ref TQ458163)

GETTING THERE:
Situated on A26 5 miles northeast of Lewes and 4 miles south of Uckfield. Alternative parking is available in Isfield itself; the walk will then be joined at point 2.

PUBLIC TRANSPORT:
Brighton & Hove Bus service 28 runs hourly between Brighton and Tunbridge Wells and stops outside The Halfway House.

1. From the rear of the car park, walk directly across a field towards a gate halfway along the opposite boundary. Continue ahead to the right of paddocks and stables, keeping to the right of the field beyond and passing to the right of a white house and tennis court. Go through a pair of gates, ignoring an intermediate gate leading off to the right, and maintain direction through a kissing gate to emerge onto a track beside a stream. When the track meets a gravel drive, bear left to reach a road (TQ452170).

2. Turn right and follow the road past Isfield station, ignoring a road on the left heading into Isfield centre. Shortly after the line of houses ends as the road bears round to the right, turn left onto a concrete drive at **Wharton's Farm** (TQ455173). Turn left again almost immediately, following a hedge on the right to reach a large field. Keep along the field's left-hand boundary to cross a bridge over the **Lavender Line.**

3. Beyond the bridge, bear right on an enclosed footpath, passing through a metal kissing gate and turning left almost immediately into a pine plantation. On emerging, continue ahead through rough grassland which narrows as it passes to the right of more paddocks. At a footpath junction at the end of the paddocks (TQ452178), turn right onto a concrete drive which passes three barns. When the path splits again, maintain direction down an unsurfaced track away from the concrete drive. As this veers left, the path enters a field and passes along its right-hand edge. Continue ahead over a stream and into the field beyond, at the corner of which the path bears right through a gap in the hedge to skirt a meander in the River Uck.

The Lavender Line; not named, as might be expected, after the flower, but more prosaically after the coal merchants A. E. Lavender & Sons who once operated from the station yard.

4. At a junction (TQ455181), ignore a path crossing left over the river and continue through a metal gate to keep the river on the left. Soon after bearing left around another meander the path passes through a metal kissing gate and then immediately right through a small patch of woodland to recross the railway line. Continue directly ahead initially through rough grassland and then climbing gradually uphill through the centre of an arable field. At the top of this, turn left down a country lane which passes **Worth Farm** and Worth Manor. When the road bears right shortly before a ford, turn left (TQ462185) and cross a bridge over a small ditch to enter the right-hand edge of a field. Follow a clear path to another bridge, this time crossing the River Uck. The path continues directly ahead, with the river meandering sharply back and forth to the left, before passing under a low bridge once carrying the Lewes-Uckfield railway line.

5. The path is now enclosed with the Uck on the left and a field on the right. This soon emerges at the head of a field with the barns passed earlier visible ahead and a brick pillbox in the foreground. This area of the Ouse Valley is known as **'Pillbox Alley'** due to the large number that were constructed here as a precaution against invasion during WWII. Turn right on an enclosed broad grassy margin

which continues along the edge of a second field and becomes a grassy track by the third. In the near corner of the fourth, go over a stile on the left and head diagonally across to a stile just before the far right corner (TQ452184), with the grand building of the Old Rectory visible to the right. Over the stile, head through a small strip of woodland and skirt the edge of a conifer plantation to reach a road opposite **Isfield Place** (TQ449184).

6. Turn left, passing the village pond before turning onto **Church Lane** towards Isfield Church. Another pillbox can be seen on the left hidden beneath ivy. When the

Dew-laced sign just beyond the village pond.

lane reaches the isolated Isfield Church, turn left through a wooden kissing gate and half double back to a wooden bridge over a small tributary leading to the River Ouse just a short distance away to the right. Over the tributary the path heads along the left-hand edge of the field beyond and over another bridge, this time over the Uck, before climbing up the centre of the following field to emerge on a road via a short enclosed path between houses.

Near Isfield Village Hall.

7. Turn right and then shortly right again on a footpath immediately before the **Village Hall** (TQ449178) and follow an enclosed path to the left of fields. Maintain direction around the left-hand edge of the field beyond to emerge onto a surfaced track. Turn left to reach Isfield Post Office and maintain direction via a footway to reach Isfield Station. This rejoins the walk at point 2.and a right turn followed by an almost immediate left down a driveway to Farm Place allows us to retrace our steps back to the start.

ISFIELD AT A GLANCE

- Isfield church, like that at Barcombe, serves to mark the location of the original village before the plague in the Middle Ages. To the west of the church is a Norman castle motte guarding the river Ouse. In the Domesday book of 1086, Isfield is recorded as 'Sifelle' and prior to this it is believed to have been owned by Earl Harold Godwin, who later became King Harold before losing his life in the Battle of Hastings in 1066.

- Dame Thora Hird once lived in Isfield and Roger Daltrey, lead singer of The Who, was famously refused a drink in the Laughing Fish when the then landlord took a dislike to him.

- Isfield station was once an unloading point for prisoners of war doing forestry work in the area. In 1912, it took 7 minutes to travel from Isfield station to Barcombe Mills, with Lewes a further 9 minutes away. Today, Isfield station marks the centre of the Lavender Line, which operates a preserved railway along a mile of the old railway. For more information see www.lavender-line.co.uk

- Much of Isfield's development can be attributed to its proximity to the River Ouse, with many building materials - together with other produce - making their way upstream from Lewes and Newhaven. Until 1857, Isfield had a flourishing Paper Mill and the adjacent lock is still discernible.

• • • • • • • • • •

Isfield station.

LEWES

SWAN INN

One of three Harveys-owned pubs in Lewes, this charming pre-Georgian coaching inn is situated in the southern suburb of Southover at the junction of Southover High Street and Kingston Road. Run by the same tenant for over thirty years, the pub features a sheltered beer garden and, on chilly days, a welcoming log fire. Alongside traditional pub fare, including Sunday roasts, there is also a delicious tapas menu.

For more information call 01273 480211.

Lewes's other Harveys tied houses can be found at The John Harvey Tavern, by the brewery itself, and at The Dorset Arms, which boasts one of Lewes' largest beer gardens, an extensive seafood menu and six comfortable en suite rooms. For more information see www.johnharveytavern.co.uk and www.thedorsetlewes.com.

THE WALK

LENGTH: 4 MILES

This gentle stroll quickly heads into the brookland of the Ouse valley, later passing beneath the scarp slope of the South Downs and through the original village centre of Kingston with its picturesque mixture of cottages and quaint Norman Church of St Pancras. Returning over Ashcombe Hollow, there are panoramic views stretching from Lewes Castle and Mount Caburn to Firle Beacon and, on a clear day, as far as Seaford Head.

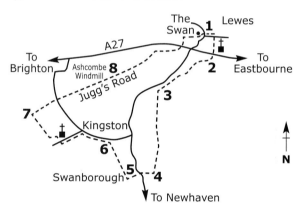

- **OS Map:**
- Explorer 122: Brighton & Hove
- **START POINT:**
- The Swan Inn (BN7 1HU; grid ref TQ408095)
- **GETTING THERE:**
- From A27 or C7 head towards Southover High Street running
- along the south edge of the town. Alternative parking is possible
- in Cockshut Road car park at point 2.
- **PUBLIC TRANSPORT:**
- Lewes is well served by trains from Brighton, Eastbourne, London
- and Seaford. Buses also operate to Uckfield and the surrounding
- district.

1. Emerging from the Swan Inn, cross immediately ahead into **Southover High Street.** A few yards after passing Anne of Cleves House, a 15th century timber-framed Wealden Hall House given to her as part of her divorce settlement with Henry VIII in 1540, turn right into **Cockshut Road** to walk soon beneath a bridge carrying the Brighton to Lewes railway line.

A turning on the left leads towards the ruins of Lewes Priory, an extensive Norman structure which was originally larger than Chichester Cathedral before suffering with the Dissolution of the Monasteries in the 1530s.

When Cockshut Road forks just beyond Southdown Sports Club, take the right turning signposted 'Access to Rise Farm only', passing through a short tunnel beneath the A27 before bearing right immediately afterwards to follow a signposted footpath through a kissing gate into Lewes Brooks.

Lewes Brooks is a 330-hectare biological Site of Special Scientific Interest on the floodplain of the River Ouse. Drained in the 18th century, some of the ditches and wetland have been restored by the RSPB and over 100 snipe now spend the winter here. The brooks are one of the few places in Sussex where lapwings and redshanks breed and the only place in the world where the Lewes Water Beetle can be found.

Looking back over Lewes Brooks towards the distinctive peak of Mount Caburn.

2. Continue ahead through another kissing gate and then turn immediately right up a small embankment to follow a clear grass path beside a drainage ditch, with Mount Caburn and Firle Beacon visible behind and the floodplains of the Ouse valley stretching away to the left. Although unmarked, the path very soon crosses the **Greenwich Meridian** line of 0° longitude, which passes only a few metres to the west of the Swan Inn itself.

View towards the South Downs above Kingston.

3. Maintain direction through another kissing gate and, ignoring a turning on the right heading towards a main road (TQ405089), the path shortly bears left to reach another kissing gate leading into an arable field. Cross through the middle of the field to a narrow hedge-lined path which briefly runs behind Lewes Garden Centre. When the path meets a driveway leading towards sewage works, turn right and then almost immediately left up a few steps and through another kissing gate, crossing half right over another arable field.

4. On reaching an isolated signpost in the middle of the field (TQ404078) there is the opportunity to look back towards the distinctive landmark of Lewes Castle before turning right towards the main road from Kingston to Newhaven. Cross over directly ahead onto a lane signposted towards Swanborough, shortly passing **Swanborough Manor,** originally a grange of Lewes Priory forming the administrative centre of the monastic farms in the area.

5. When the lane forks at a Y-junction (TQ401077), take the right-hand option, following a surfaced track between farm buildings. After passing Downlands house, maintain direction through a gate to pass paddocks, with Swanborough Hill and the South Downs Way looming up some 600ft high on the left. Continue along a hedge-lined path with a view of Ashcombe Windmill straight ahead.

6. On meeting a main road (TQ398083), turn left towards Kingston, turning left onto **The Street** after 175 yards when the main road bears round to the right. After a short distance, the flint-walled village pound where stray sheep were once kept can be seen on the left. Immediately after passing the quaint Norman church of St Pancras, turn right through a gate onto a surfaced path past the churchyard which bears left around a recreation ground and tennis courts before leading into Church Lane. Maintain direction as the road surface becomes more uneven and then starts to climb uphill, narrowing to a path before meeting a footpath T-junction (TQ387086).

7. Turn right down **Jugg's Road,** an ancient route which ran from Brighton and was used to carry fish to Lewes market - the fish were kept fresh or salted in pottery jugs, hence the name. When this reaches the main road (TQ390087), cross directly ahead on a driveway signposted 'Footpath to Ashcombe' (still a continuation of the original Jugg's Road). The driveway shortly narrows to a gravel track before passing through a gate into open grassland by **Ashcombe Windmill,** a recently restored replica of the original six-sweep post mill which was destroyed during a gale in 1916.

8. Maintain direction on a well-trodden grass path, later passing through a gate onto a tree-lined gravel path which leads onto a lane. Follow the lane downhill and over a high bridge crossing the A27 and Lewes to Brighton railway line. On the far side pass beside a very small park to soon emerge by the main road to Kingston, with the Swan Inn a few paces away on the left.

Looking eastwards over the Ouse valley towards Mount Caburn and Firle Beacon.

LEWES AT A GLANCE

- With a population of 16,000, Lewes is the county town of East Sussex. Occupying a strategic position above the Ouse valley, Lewes derives its name from the Anglo-Saxon word 'hlaew' meaning hill, a hill on which the Norman fortification of Lewes Castle dominates.

- Tom Paine, author of *Rights of Man* and advocate of American independence, lived in Bull House on Lewes High Street between 1768 and 1774. Modernist writer and Bloomsbury Group member Virginia Woolf purchased Monk's House, her weekend cottage in nearby Rodmell, in an auction at The White Hart Hotel for the princely sum of £700 in 1919.

- The scale of Lewes' Guy Fawkes celebrations is unique in England, arising from the outburst of anti-Catholicism that followed the Gunpowder Plot of 1605. Bonfire processions parade the streets with blazing tar barrels and elaborate effigies before leading to one of six bonfire sites, all competing for the best firework display.

- Lewes has its own complementary currency, The Lewes Pound, which can be used alongside pounds Sterling. Launched to support local producers and traders and to raise awareness of the importance of shopping locally, The Lewes Pound functions as a voucher or token redeemable for many goods or services within the town. For more information see www.thelewespound.org.

·········

Processions at Lewes Bonfire Night.

PLUMPTON GREEN

PLOUGH

Replacing the original Plough Inn which was demolished to make way for the runway of RAF Chailey during WWII, the pub today is actually located a few yards to the south of its ancestor. The airfield itself has now returned to agricultural use, but a memorial in The Plough's grounds commemorates those Polish servicemen who manned spitfires there between 1944-5 and serves to remind visitors of the pub's heritage.

Run by the Turner family, The Plough is a busy country pub with a patio and a large attractive beer garden. An extensive selection of local food and drink is on offer, including a delicious homemade cottage pie made with Harveys Old Ale.

For more information see www.theploughatplumpton.co.uk or call 01273 890 311.

THE WALK

LENGTH: 4 MILES

An undemanding walk exploring the heart of the Low Weald, passing through an attractive patchwork of fields, small woodland and ancient droving roads between the parishes of Plumpton, Streat and Westmeston. Extensive views of the South Downs can be enjoyed for much of the route, with a brief glimpse towards the High Weald near its end.

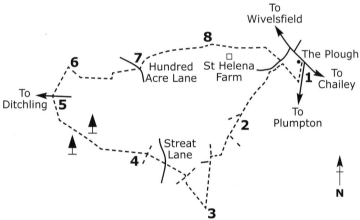

- **OS MAP:**
  Explorer 122: Brighton & Hove

- **START POINT:**
  The Plough Inn (BN7 3DF; grid ref TQ366182)

- **GETTING THERE:**
  Via B2112 or B2116 about 3 miles northeast of Ditchling at Plumpton Crossways.

- **PUBLIC TRANSPORT:**
  Countryliner bus service 166 from Lewes, Wivelsfield and Haywards Heath operates Mon-Sat and stops outside The Plough. Plumpton itself is well served by trains from Eastbourne, Seaford and London main line destinations.

1. Leaving The Plough, walk down the road towards **Plumpton Green,** turning right after 100 yards over a stile leading into a small field and crossing diagonally to the top right-hand corner to meet **St Helena Lane** (TQ363183). Turn left for 100 yards and, when the road bears round to the right, take the track on the left past Inholmes Cottage and up a small rise into woodland. Maintain direction past Copse Cottage as the track narrows into a footpath, pressing ahead through the edge of the woodland.

2. Continue through the woodland as the path begins to descend, bearing round to the right behind the corner of a field to reach a T-junction (TQ357173). Turn left through a metal gate, passing by the right of farm buildings towards an unmade track. Crossing this, maintain direction through a narrow strip of grassland bordered by hedgerows, once an ancient droving route linking the Low Weald with pastures on the South Downs.

3. About 10 yards before reaching the picturesque **Shergolds Farm** on the left, take a footpath to the right (TQ356168) over a stile into a small field. Cross this field and the next, aiming towards a gate between barns and passing to the right of a secluded pond. Beyond the barns, turn right onto a drive leading to Dean's Farm and then almost immediately left into another field which is crossed diagonally to meet **Streat Lane** (TQ353172). Maintain direction, crossing the lane into another field and keeping along its left-hand edge to reach Kent's Lane.

Like the grassland leading to Shergolds Farm and the now surfaced Streat Lane, Kent's Lane is one of many ancient droveways in the

Low Weald. The hedge and the ditch on the east side also mark the boundary line between the parishes of Streat to the east and Westmeston to the west.

Looking south along the droveway beside Shergolds Farm.

4. Turn left through a wooden gate and then immediately right to follow a path through woodland, which later reveals a stunning vista of the Downs with the Eastbourne to London railway line in the foreground. The path curves up through **Blackbrook Wood,** an ancient woodland saved from destruction by developers in the 1990s with the help of the Wildlife Trust, and is clearly marked all the way to **Middleton Common Lane** (TQ341178).

5. Cross this onto a driveway signposted 'Bridleway to Wivelsfield Green', briefly following the Sussex Border Path. When the driveway ends, continue ahead for a few yards through a brief stretch of mixed woodland to meet a footpath on the right shortly before a Y-junction (TQ343182).

6. Briefly turning back on itself, the path quickly crosses a stile into rough grassland. Turn through a large gap in the hedgerow which shortly appears on the left, heading eastwards on an enclosed strip of grassland and maintaining direction along the right-hand edge of the field beyond. On reaching the far corner by a house, ignore a gap in the hedge ahead and turn left for 75 yards to reach a stile (TQ347182). Walk along the left-hand edge of the adjacent field, passing the attractive house of Greenacres to reach **Hundred Acre Lane.**

7. Crossing the lane, head diagonally left across a small meadow and over the driveway of Huntswood House to a stile just beyond a large willow tree. Head directly opposite towards a stile halfway along the field's east boundary and maintain direction across three further fields, once part of Streat Common, a vast expanse of open land enclosed in the mid-17th century.

8. In the corner of the last of these fields, cross two stiles separated by a bridge over a ditch and climb up a short incline to meet a field with a barn, part of **St Helena Farm,** visible in the far corner. Head over a stile just to the left of the barn, maintaining direction across the next two fields towards a white house in the left-hand corner of the second. From here the High Weald can now be glimpsed on the left. Follow the fenced path to the left of the white house to reach a driveway and turn left to re-emerge onto **St Helena Lane.** Cross the field opposite to return to The Plough.

PLUMPTON GREEN AT A GLANCE

- The villages of Plumpton Green and Plumpton, two miles to the south of the former, derive their names from the Old English 'plumpt' meaning 'positioned under', referring to the villages' position 'under' the South Downs.

View of South Downs from The Gallops.

- Plumpton Green is rumoured to have been the inspiration for the popular British children's television series Trumpton, with nearby Chailey appearing as Chigley and Wivelsfield Green as Camberwick Green. Creator Gordon Murray has himself admitted that the fictional villages are representative of real locations which are 'one-and-a-half miles from each other in an equidistant triangle', although there has never been any definite confirmation.

- Plumpton Place, an elegant moated manor to the south, was originally inhabited by the Mascall family, one of whom is said, in the time of Henry VIII, to have introduced carp and the pippin apple to England. In the 1970s, Led Zeppelin guitarist Jimmy Page purchased the manor, and the credits for *In Through the Out Door,* the last album to be recorded before the death of drummer John Bonham in 1980, indicate that album mixing was done here.

• • • • • • • • • •

SEVEN STARS

Built as a Wealden Hall House around 1400, though altered in the 16th Century and re-faced in the 19th Century, The Seven Stars Inn is a Grade II listed building. The name itself is the subject of debate; perhaps referring to the crown of the Virgin Mary, or perhaps a reference to the constellation Ursa Major, or the Plough, an important symbol in a rural arable area.

It is believed that Horace Walpole stayed here in the mid-1750s and was surprised to find it was the haunt of smugglers, highwaymen, prostitutes and other 'ne'er-do-wells'. Today, The Seven Stars Inn is listed as one of the Top Ten Haunted Pubs in England with alleged experiences including phantom footsteps, shadowy apparitions and dogs reacting to sights unseen. On Sundays the pub hosts a popular carvery for which booking is essential. For more information see www.seven7stars.co.uk or call 01580 880 333.

THE WALK

LENGTH: 4.75 MILES

Exploring both sides of the Rother valley, the route quickly heads into the rolling Wealden countryside above the village before descending to the quaint hamlet of Salehurst. After crossing the river Rother itself, much of the journey lies on quiet and level country lanes, with an extensive panorama back over the valley.

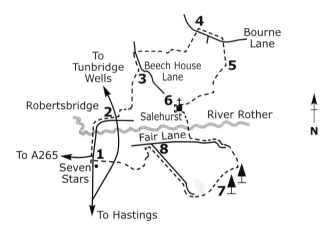

- **OS MAP:**
- Explorer 136: High Weald
- **START POINT:**
- The Seven Stars (TN32 5AJ; grid ref TQ738235)
- **GETTING THERE:**
- Via A265 or A21 ten miles north of Hastings. There is a public car park in Station Road (grid ref. TQ737236).
- **PUBLIC TRANSPORT:**
- Robertsbridge railway station is on the main line from Hastings and is 500 yards from the pub. Rider bus service 304/305 runs between Hastings and Hawkhurst (with a guaranteed bus connection to Tunbridge Wells) and stops virtually outside The Seven Stars.

1. Leaving The Seven Stars, turn right along the High Street, which contains a large number of Wealden Hall Houses from the 14th and 15th centuries. Cross a tributary of the River Rother and then the Rother itself, near which there are signs of a dismantled railway. The Rother Valley Railway aims one day to restore this line between Robertsbridge and nearby Bodiam, which is the current western extent of the popular Kent & East Sussex Railway.

2. Shortly after the road bears round to the right, turn left onto **Northbridge Street** and, as this bears left, pass by a small parking area to emerge by pedestrian traffic lights which cross the A21 (TQ740242). On the other side, turn immediately left onto a narrow surfaced path which soon bears right alongside a conifer hedge. Maintain direction as this joins a quiet residential road and, shortly before this ends, turn left onto another surfaced path which heads uphill towards a large wooden gate into **Springfield Wood** (TQ743244). Continue directly ahead, ignoring a second path heading northwest, and follow the right hand edge of the sloping field beyond to emerge onto **Beech House Lane.**

3. Turn left and when the lane begins to bear round to the left by **Oak Farm Oast** (TQ744250), follow a narrow enclosed path initially to the right of a gravel drive to emerge in the top corner of a field. Follow the right-hand edge downhill and over a stile, now following the left-hand edge of the large field beyond. In the far corner, the path crosses a small wooded stream before climbing uphill, again keeping to the left-hand field edge. On meeting a signpost halfway up the hill (TQ749252), turn right along the top of a slight embankment and then down steps to cross another wooded stream. Over this, there is a brief steep uphill climb following a line of oak trees, at the end of which the path bears left on a banked tree-lined path to pass a pond. The way then crosses a stile by a metal gate before passing through a strip of woodland

Jollies Farm Oast.

beside a further pond and emerging via an enclosed footpath onto a country lane by Jollies Farm Oast.

4. Turn right and follow the road along the top of a ridge. At a triangular junction, maintain direction onto **Bourne Lane,** turning right by Lake Abbot (TQ756253). Keep straight ahead as the route initially follows a gravel driveway, then passes under an archway and immediately to the right of a large pond before emerging through a low metal gate onto another lane. Follow the footpath signs directing right and then almost immediately left through a wooden gate to pass along the left-hand edge of a field and a small orchard. Beyond this, a surfaced drive leads downhill for a few yards until a sign directs the path over a stile into a small fenced field directly ahead.

5. In the bottom right corner of the field, bear right and follow the edge of enclosed woodland to meet a grassy track. Maintain direction, soon with a small stream visible in a dip to the right. The track emerges along the right-hand edge of a large arable field, from which **Salehurst Church** can be seen directly ahead. When this emerges by a lane (TQ753245), turn right and then immediately left through a metal gate, passing along the right-hand edge of two further fields. In the far corner of the second of these, turn left and then in a few paces right through a metal kissing gate between two large oak trees. Walk through the centre of a churchyard and to the left of the church itself to reach the village of Salehurst.

6. Turn left and follow a track downhill round the bottom edge of the churchyard. When this bears right, follow the path to the left of a converted oast and downhill on a railed path which soon crosses the fast-flowing River Rother. When the path reaches **Fair Lane** (TQ751238) turn left and follow the lane as it winds round to the right near where Robertsbridge Abbey was once located, although little remains today except foundations and part of the abbot's residence (now a private house). Shortly after passing attractive oast houses turn right on an enclosed path which skirts round a farm to emerge onto a driveway (TQ757237). Turn right and continue directly ahead as the path itself enters the edge of a woodland and begins to climb uphill, soon turning westwards.

7. At the end of the woodland, ignore a path heading left and continue directly ahead downhill to meet a track. Maintain direction again as the track crosses a river and soon passes to the left of a large pond, becoming surfaced shortly after another track joins from the left (TQ751232). Very shortly take a surfaced driveway on the left which loops round the attractive **Salehurst Park Farm,** passing two converted oast houses and another pond. From here, the drive becomes a quiet lane with open views through the low Rother valley.

8. When the lane meets **Russet Farm** (TQ746237), turn left and then, just past a wooden gate, left again towards the corner of Park Wood. Turn right on a clear but narrow path and then right again at a cross track after 50 yards (TQ744235). On emerging from the wood the path passes downhill beside sewage works before crossing a stream and climbing directly ahead to the top corner where a wooded path leads round to a bridge crossing the A21. Once over the bridge, follow the lane directly ahead to emerge onto the High Street immediately beside The Seven Stars.

Looking towards Robertsbridge and Salehurst church.

ROBERTSBRIDGE AT A GLANCE

- Robertsbridge was within the area controlled by the Hawkhurst gang, the notorious gang of smugglers who operated in the South East between 1735 and 1749. In 1740, at Silver Hill (just under 2 miles north of Robertsbridge), Revenue Officer Thomas Carswell was shot and killed by the Hawkhurst gang while he was carrying 750kg of recovered contraband tea to Hastings.

- The very first Cub Scout Pack was started in Robertsbridge by Baden-Powell in 1916, nine years after the foundation of the Scouts, in order to cater for the younger boys who wanted to take part in scouting but were not yet old enough. Baden-Powell himself spent a time in nearby Ewhurst Place from 1913.

- In the mid-19th century, a music manuscript containing the earliest surviving music written for keyboard was found among records of Robertsbridge Abbey. Dating from around 1360, the so-called Robertsbridge Codex is now located in the British Library.

- Robertsbridge is also renowned for the manufacture of cricket bats, started by L.J. Nicolls in 1876 and continuing to this day. These cricket bats were used by W.G. Grace to achieve his record-breaking 100th century in 1894.

•••••••••

Footpath sign by Fair Lane.

DORSET ARMS

The Dorset Arms dates back to the 15th century, when it was used as a farmhouse. Lying in the valley of the River Medway in the heart of the High Weald, the Dorset Arms has been serving the local community for well over two hundred years, boasting original flagstone floors, timber ceiling beams, attractive casement windows and a huge open fireplace ideal for the colder months.

An extensive menu and wine list is supplemented by four blackboards of specials often including an excellent steak and ale pie and, on the dessert selection, a home-grown spiced apple pie and a strawberry pavlova.

For further information see www.dorset-arms.co.uk or call 01892 770 278.

THE WALK

LENGTH: 3.75 MILES

Traversing both sides of the river Medway, this delightful stroll passes through a series of gently undulating fields to reach Hartfield. After an optional detour to visit Pooh Corner, the route resumes by Hartfield Church, striking out across the line of a dismantled railway and following the course of the river Medway before joining a quiet country lane to return to the start.

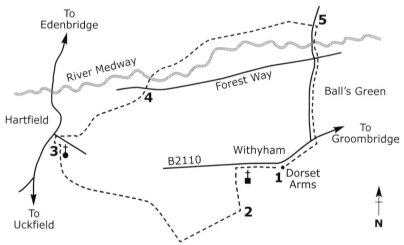

- **OS MAP:**
  Explorer 135: Ashdown Forest
- **START POINT:**
  The Dorset Arms (TN7 4BD; grid ref TQ496357)
- **GETTING THERE:**
  Via B2110 from Hartfield or Groombridge four miles north of Crowborough. There is limited on-street parking in Ball's Green and Hartfield.
- **PUBLIC TRANSPORT:**
  Metrobus 291 between Crawley and Tunbridge Wells leaves hourly from the Dorset Arms.

1. Turn left to follow a footway beside the B2110, initially on the right side of the road and then the left. As the road bears left downhill after 200 yards, head through a gate marked **Buckhurst Estate.** *This was once owned by Thomas Sackville, ancestor of Vita Sackville-West and writer of Gorboduc (1561), the first English drama to be written in blank verse. Queen Elizabeth I visited and hunted at Buckhurst and the royal connection has been continued by Queen Victoria, King Edward VII, Queen Elizabeth II and the late Princess Margaret who all visited and planted trees here. Continue uphill along a private drive, passing Withyham Church and observing a large lake visible in the valley to the right.*

2. Immediately after a driveway to **Forstal Cottage** (TQ493353), turn right, following the High Weald Landscape Trail on a clearly marked path passing to the left of large trees in the centre of a field to enter a small woodland. When the path forks, bear right and continue through the woodland, following signs over a bridge. Follow the right-hand edge of the field beyond beside paddocks, passing through a gateway and bearing left uphill. After reaching a second gateway, cross diagonally through the centre of a field towards a fingerpost in the middle of a line of trees (TQ482356). Beyond this, continue through the centre of the next field, keeping the tall spire of Hartfield Church on the right. The path then follows the right-hand edge of two further fields to emerge by the church itself.

From here it is well worth extending the walk by keeping ahead into the village of Hartfield itself

Hartfield Church.

which contains a number of attractive tile-hung and half-timbered buildings. Like Withyham, the village lies on the north edge of the Ashdown Forest, whose one-time status as a royal deer hunting park can be discerned in the name of Hartfield: the field of harts (i.e. male deer). Hartfield is perhaps most famous for its connection with the Winnie the Pooh stories written by A. A. Milne at the beginning of the 20th century. Once on the High Street, Pooh Corner gift shop and tearoom is a short distance away on the left (TQ477356), while the infamous Poohsticks bridge can be found about 1.5 miles to the south of the village itself (TQ470339).

3. Turn left and then very shortly right to pass under an archway leading along the left-hand edge of the churchyard and then along a surfaced path through a meadow. At the end of this, turn right and then almost immediately left onto a road signed **Castlefields** (leading to Motte Field). Follow this as it bears round to the right and then immediately after passing a parking area, turn left along a tarmac path leading to another meadow. Skirt around the right-hand edge of a mound (TQ482360), the remains of a one-time fortification, and then pass over a stream and left into the bottom

Looking towards Summerford Farm.

edge of a large field. Continue along the bottom edge of this and the field beyond, in which the path cuts through a gap along its left-hand boundary before crossing diagonally right towards a dismantled railway line. This is the Forest Way, a ten-mile trail between East Grinstead and Groombridge running along the route of a dismantled railway, the line of which can be clearly identified by the raised embankment directly ahead.

4. Cross the **Forest Way** (TQ487363) and then over the river Medway by a footbridge before skirting to the left of trees hiding a pond. As the way forks, ignore a path heading uphill, turning right alongside the edge of the woodland and then along the left-hand edge of a meadow. From here, the route is easily identifiable all the way to **Summerford Farm,** whose three converted oast houses can be clearly seen on the approach. The path emerges onto the tarmac path to Summerford Farm before passing a number of attractive houses to reach a country road (TQ498367).

5. Turn right along the road to recross the river Medway. Soon the road also crosses the Forest Way by the site of the old Withyham station, the platform of which can still be seen although now part of a private house. The road leads uphill into the attractive village of **Ball's Green** before reaching a T-junction opposite **Duckings Farm** (TQ499358). Turn right to follow a footway beside the B2110 to return to the Dorset Arms.

Looking towards Summerford Farm.

WITHYHAM AT A GLANCE

• Withyham is thought most likely to have been founded for the workers on the Buckhurst estate. The station, actually located closer to the hamlet of Ball's Green, closed in 1967 as a result of the Beeching Axe. The former trackbed has been largely restored as the Forest Way cycle and footpath from Groombridge to East Grinstead, where it connects to the Worth Way to run to Three Bridges. At Groombridge, a section of the line has been restored by the Spa Valley Railway: for details see www.spavalleyrailway.co.uk

• Withyham village features in the short story 'The Horror of the Heights' by Sir Arthur Conan Doyle as the finding place of the Joyce-Armstrong Fragment, a supposedly real fragment of a diary detailing the airborne adventures of the author of the diary.

• In 1680 the Sackville Chapel was built within Withyham church, containing many monuments to the family. In 1962, after the death of Vita Sackville-West, the author who rebuilt the gardens at Sissinghurst, her ashes were placed in the Sackville family crypt.

• • • • • • • • • •

Above Buckhurst Estate.

THE HARVEY HOP

Harveys owns a great variety of pubs throughout Sussex and even a few beyond. Many people have undertaken a journey known as 'The Harvey Hop', visiting all 47 pubs: any Harvey pub will stamp the 'Harvey Hop' passport after purchasing any pint or bottle of Harveys. A completed passport will be redeemed for a prestigious item exclusive to Harvey Hoppers.

Harveys pubs in Sussex not featured in this current collection:

- **Brighton** - Constant Service
- **Brighton** - Mitre Tavern
- **Crawley** - White Hart
- **Crowborough** - Wheatsheaf

- **Eastbourne** - Arlington Arms
- **Eastbourne** - Hurst Arms
- **Eastbourne** - Terminus
- **Eastbourne** - Victoria
- **Five Ash Down** (nr. Uckfield) - Pig & Butcher
- **Golden Cross** - Golden Cross Inn
- **Hailsham** - Grenadier
- **Hailsham** - Kings Head
- **Haywards Heath** - Heath

- **Hove** - Poet's Corner
- **Midhurst** - Swan Inn
- **Polegate** - Dinkum
- **Stone Cross** (nr. Pevensey)- Red Lion
- **Turners Hill** - Red Lion
- **Uckfield** - Alma Arms

Kent

- **Bells Yew Green** (nr Frant) - Brecknock Arms
- **Chipstead** (nr. Sevenoaks) - Bricklayers Arms
- **Cowden** (nr. Edenbridge) - Fountain
- **Hadlow** - Two Brewers
- **Lamberhurst** - Elephants Head
- **Maidstone** - Pilot

Surrey

- **Redhill** - Garland

Further afield

- **London SE1**- Royal Oak
- **Rogate** (Hampshire) - White Horse
- **Sunningdale** (Berkshire) - Nags Head